WORLD HISTORY
THE HUMAN EXPERIENCE

Geography and History Activities

NATIONAL GEOGRAPHIC SOCIETY

Mounir A. Farah
Andrea Berens Karls

GLENCOE
McGraw-Hill

New York, New York   Columbus, Ohio   Woodland Hills, California   Peoria, Illinois

Customize Your Resources

No matter how you organize your teaching resources, Glencoe has what you need.

The **Teacher's Classroom Resources** for *World History: The Human Experience* provides you with a wide variety of supplemental materials to enhance the classroom experience. These resources appear as individual booklets accompanied by a file management kit of file folders, labels, and tabbed binder dividers in a carryall file box. The booklets are designed to open flat so that pages can be easily photocopied without removing them from their booklets. However, if you choose to create separate files, the pages are perforated for easy removal. You may customize these materials using our file folders or tabbed dividers.

The individual booklets and the file management kit supplied in **Teacher's Classroom Resources** give you the flexibility to organize these resources in a combination that best suits your teaching style. Below are several alternatives:

- **Organize all resources by category**
  (all Tests, all Geography and History Activities, all History Simulations, and so on, filed separately)
- **Organize resources by category and chapter**
  (all Chapter 1 activities, all Chapter 1 tests, etc.)
- **Organize resources sequentially by lesson**
  (activities, quizzes, study guides, etc., for Section 1, Section 2, and so on)

Glencoe/McGraw-Hill
A Division of The McGraw·Hill Companies

Copyright © by the McGraw-Hill Companies, Inc. All rights reserved. Permission is granted to reproduce the material contained herein on the condition that such material be reproduced only for classroom use; be provided to students, teachers, and families without charge; and be used solely in conjunction with *World History: The Human Experience*. Any other reproduction, for use or sale, is prohibited without prior written permission of the publisher.

Send all inquiries:
Glencoe/McGraw-Hill
936 Eastwind Drive
Westerville, OH 43081

ISBN 0-02-823225-9

Printed in the United States of America
5 6 7 8 9 10   045   02 01 00 99

GEOGRAPHY AND HISTORY ACTIVITIES

TABLE OF CONTENTS

To the Teacher iv
Chapter 1 Human-Environment Interaction: *Sumerian City Planning* 1
Chapter 2 Location: *The Huang River* 3
Chapter 3 Place: *The Bees of Carthage* 5
Chapter 4 Location: *Lost Atlantis* 7
Chapter 5 Region: *The Greek Language* 9
Chapter 6 Movement: *Roman Roads* 11
Chapter 7 Place: *The Discovery of Jenne-jeno* 13
Chapter 8 Place: *Monsoons of India* 15
Chapter 9 Region: *The Silk Road* 17
Chapter 10 Place: *Constantinople* 19
Chapter 11 Human-Environment Interaction: *Bedouin Life* 21
Chapter 12 Movement: *Vikings* 23
Chapter 13 Human-Environment Interaction: *Gothic Cathedrals* 25
Chapter 14 Location: *Strait of Malacca* 27
Chapter 15 Human-Environment Interaction: *What's for Dinner?* 29
Chapter 16 Movement: *Venice, Queen of the Adriatic* 31
Chapter 17 Location: *Columbus's Landfall* 33
Chapter 18 Region: *In the Shogun's Grip* 35
Chapter 19 Human-Environment Interaction: *Dutch Masters* 37
Chapter 20 Location: *Where Is the World?* 39
Chapter 21 Region: *Looking at the Land* 41
Chapter 22 Movement: *A Doomed March to Russia* 43
Chapter 23 Human-Environment Interaction: *A Big Ditch or a Grand Canal?* 45
Chapter 24 Place: *Population Time Bomb* 47
Chapter 25 Region: *From Convict Colony to Commonwealth* 49
Chapter 26 Place: *Russia* 51
Chapter 27 Movement: *Railroads in India* 53
Chapter 28 Human-Environment Interaction: *The Battle of the Somme* 55
Chapter 29 Location: *Jews in Europe* 57
Chapter 30 Region: *East Africa* 59
Chapter 31 Movement: *The Blockade of Japan* 61
Chapter 32 Region: *The Bipolar World* 63
Chapter 33 Place: *Hong Kong* 65
Chapter 34 Movement: *South African Apartheid* 67
Chapter 35 Human-Environment Interaction: *Disaster in Kuwait* 69
Chapter 36 Movement: *Mexico City* 71
Chapter 37 Human-Environment Interaction: *Forests on Fire* 73
Answer Key 75
Acknowledgments 84

To the Teacher

The curved prow of a Viking warship grinds ashore on a lonely beach. Centuries later, an Indian gentleman burns the clothes he wore on the inaugural trip of the British railway line in his country. In 1991 explosions rip through Kuwaiti oil fields, sending black clouds into the choking skies. These dramas and many others set the stage for students to explore the five themes of geography.

Geography and History Activities reinforce the National Geographic Society's five basic themes by applying them to the people, places, and events in world history. The introduction to each activity draws students into the lesson and links it to familiar content in the corresponding chapter of *World History: The Human Experience.* The first page of the lesson uses primary sources and a variety of visuals to explore an interesting topic. This topic becomes a springboard for teaching a specific geography theme on the second page. Questions assess understanding of the theme. Critical thinking exercises and activities help students continue their study of the topic and apply it to their own lives.

Answers to the activities are provided at the back of the booklet.

The Five Themes of Geography and History

Location: *Position on the Earth's Surface*
Location can be identified in absolute and relative terms. Absolute location pinpoints a position using a reference system such as latitude and longitude. Understanding relative location can lead to a better understanding of why people chose a particular location for settlement.

Place: *Physical and Human Characteristics*
Just as every individual has a unique personality, so does every place. The "place" lessons investigate the physical and human features that give an area its identity. Students analyze characteristics of places using a variety of information sources, such as maps, tables, graphs, photos, and personal accounts.

Human-Environment Interaction: *Relationships Within Places*
People respond to and modify their environments to meet their needs and wants. The ways in which people have responded to their environments have varied. Increasingly sophisticated technology has given all cultures greater control over their environment, but it also raises the specter of devastating damage to the environment.

Movement: *Humans Interacting on the Earth*
Places are connected by the movement of people, ideas, and resources. For centuries people, ideas, and resources have moved between places, whether it was along the Silk Road or shipping lanes. Modern transportation and communication have helped make cultures more interdependent, but barriers to movement still exist.

Regions: *How They Change and Form*
The basic unit of geographic study is the region, an area that shares common characteristics. Organizing information by regions helps students learn more about people and land. These lessons explore regions ranging from areas of Hellenistic culture to tropical rain forests.

Name _____ Date _____ Class _____

GEOGRAPHY and HISTORY Activity 1

Human-Environment Interaction: *Sumerian City Planning*

The first cities built by the ancient river valley civilizations, with their storehouses of food and treasures, often were tempting targets for their neighbors. How could a city defend itself against raiding nomadic bands and the armies of competing cities?

Ancient city dwellers in the valley of the Tigris and Euphrates Rivers faced the danger of catastrophic floods, invasions by their enemies, and attacks by hungry citizens of outlying areas. Building walls, then, was crucial to the defense of the first cities, and all Sumerian cities—including Ur, Uruk, and Eridu—were walled. Of all the heroic deeds of Gilgamesh, the god-king of Sumerian epic, building the walls around Uruk—probably about 2700 B.C.—was his mightiest achievement. His people slaved for decades building more than 8 miles (almost 13 kilometers) of city walls with more than 900 semicircular turrets.

Sumerian workers constructed the inner core of their walls from millions of sun-dried bricks made from river mud, and they used kiln-baked clay slabs as weather-resistant overlay. The walls, mortared with asphalt, reached as high as 20 feet (6 meters) in places. To prevent walls from trapping water after heavy rains or floods, the Sumerians built a system of clay pipes in the foundations to drain the water.

The Gilgamesh Epic

Gilgamesh . . . built a wall around his city to make it safe against attack. Its pinnacles shone like brass. Its outer surface was armored with stone cladding [facing], every brick had been hardened in the fire. The people of Uruk groaned beneath the burden of the building of the wall, for Gilgamesh drove them on without pity. . . . The drums that summoned the people to work were sounded without a pause, so that the son had no time to spend with his father, nor the lover with his lady.

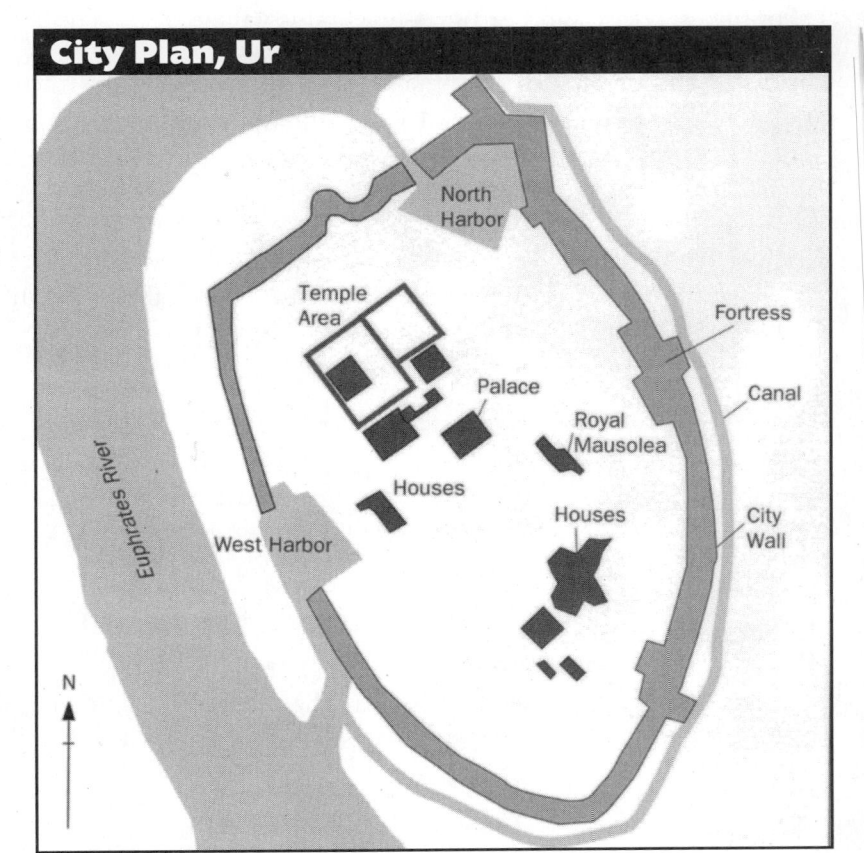

City Plan, Ur

Between the time of its first settlement next to the Euphrates River around 4500 B.C. and its total abandonment in the 300s B.C., the Sumerian city of Ur was rebuilt and restored several times. This plan reflects the city in about 1800 B.C.

World History — Geography and History Activities 1

Name _____ Date _____ Class _____

GEOGRAPHY and HISTORY Activity 1

Focus on Human-Environment Interaction

The people of the earliest civilizations chose to settle on the flood plains of river valleys because of the fertile soils, water resources, and opportunities for transportation. This natural environment had its disadvantages, too—for example, periodic floods. In order to survive and flourish, the early civilizations learned how to modify their environment by building dikes, canals, dams, and reservoirs, both for flood control and for irrigation.

When people built cities, they also modified their natural environment. With its natural surfaces built on and built up, the physical environment of a city was very much a creation of its people. A walled city, its residents hoped, would be safe.

1. Why do people try to change their natural environment?

2. What does their brickmaking suggest about how the Sumerians adapted to the available resources in their environment?

3. What does the building of the city walls reveal about the political system and technological levels of the early cities in the Tigris-Euphrates valley?

4. What features of the plan of Ur, other than the city walls, show how its people modified their environment?

Critical Thinking

5. **Determining Cause and Effect** Around 2000 B.C., the population of Ur—within the city walls and in the surrounding suburbs—may have exceeded 20,000. How might this concentration of people have created environmental problems?

6. **Making Comparisons** Even as agricultural settlements in river valleys evolved into the first cities, neighboring peoples continued their nomadic way of life. Contrast the way nomadic peoples related to their environment with the way farming societies did.

Activity

7. With your classmates, brainstorm a list of the problems an urban planner must consider in designing a modern city. In what ways are these problems similar to those faced by the planners of the first cities? In what ways are the problems of modern cities different?

GEOGRAPHY and HISTORY Activity 2

Location: *The Huang River*

A cartographer draws a map showing the boundaries of ancient Chinese dynasties. She will certainly include the Huang River, the cradle of Chinese civilization. But if she shows today's path of the river on her historical map, will it be accurate?

With more than a billion tons of fine, yellow silt flowing downriver annually from the Loess Plateau along a twisting route of right angle bends, the riverbed of the Huang continuously builds up. Over the centuries, disastrous floods have ruptured protective dikes and inundated the North China Plain, often resulting in changes to the course of the Huang River.

The source of the Huang is in the eastern highlands of Tibet, at an altitude of about 15,000 feet (457 meters). After descending rugged gorges, it crosses a plateau and then falls again to a flat lower basin. Along the lower stretch, much of the riverbed sits above the surrounding farmland. When raging waters cut through dikes, floods can injure millions and bury whole villages with silt.

Changes in the Huang River's course during the past several thousand years have caused the point where the river enters the Yellow Sea to vary by as much as 500 miles (800 kilometers). A cartographer who wants to be historically accurate must determine the exact location of the river at a given time.

For example, from 2278 to 602 B.C., the Huang River took a northerly route, flowing through the city of Tianjin to enter nearby Bo Hai. From 602 B.C. to A.D. 70, the Huang River and its mouth shifted to the south of Shandong Peninsula, but from A.D. 70 to 1048, the river again shifted north.

The Changing Course of the Huang River

The present location of the mouth of the Huang River reflects a significant change that occurred in 1858. For the prior 500 years, the river had followed the "Old Course."

Name .... Date .... Class ....

GEOGRAPHY and HISTORY Activity 2

Focus on Location

The absolute, or exact, location of a place can be determined by its coordinates on a map grid of north-south meridians (longitude lines) and east-west parallels (latitude lines). Degrees of longitude give the distance of any place east or west of the Prime Meridian, and degrees of latitude give its distance north or south of the Equator. The coordinates for any point on the map, then, are a pair of numbers giving the latitude and longitude.

To draw a river on a map, a cartographer must be able to locate every point along the river's course exactly on the map's grid. At present the Huang River enters the Bo Hai at about 38°N latitude and 119°E longitude.

1. What information do you need in order to give the absolute location of a place?

2. What was the absolute location of the mouth of the Huang River during the years it was located near Tianjin?

3. What was the absolute location of the mouth of the Huang River when it was located on the Old Course south of Shandong?

4. Changes in the course of the Huang River occurred abruptly. What events probably took place in 602 B.C. and A.D. 70?

Critical Thinking

5. **Predicting Consequences** The Indus River has shifted its course over the centuries. What might have been the consequences of these changes to the Harappan civilization?

6. **Making Inferences** The Huang River was given its name, which means "yellow," because of the yellow loess suspended in its waters. Why is the Huang River nicknamed "China's Sorrow"?

Activity

7. Serious floods have been part of the history of the Mississippi River. Using a map of the United States, determine the absolute location of the headwaters (river's source) and delta of the Mississippi River, as well as of its key river ports. Then research the efforts that have been made since 1900 to control the Mississippi flooding.

Name .... Date .... Class ....

GEOGRAPHY and HISTORY Activity 3

Place: *The Bees of Carthage*

When Dido, queen of the Phoenician city-state of Tyre, offered colorful baubles for as much land as an oxhide could cover, the North Africans eagerly agreed. They did not foresee that the great city of Carthage would rise on the patch of land they had just traded. How did the Tyrians turn their bargain into a thriving commercial center?

According to legend, Dido cut the oxhide into strips and encircled a hilltop and a harbor. There she and her fellow Phoenicians founded Carthage—the "New City"—about 750 B.C.

The Phoenician settlers of Carthage picked a strategic location at a choke point of the Mediterranean. The physical features of the location—an easily defensible peninsula with an excellent harbor—were also promising. The new feature added to the physical geography was human—the influx of settlers from Tyre. Fleeing from political disturbances and Assyrian attacks on Tyre, the settlers swelled the population of Carthage until, at its height, it numbered some 500,000. A later Roman poet, Virgil, described the thronging Tyrians as they built their new city and compared them to a swarm of busy bees. These "bees" soon turned a bit of desert shore bought with trinkets into the hub of a trading empire.

Virgil's *Aeneid*

The eager men of Tyre work steadily: some build the city walls or citadel—they roll up stones by hand; some select the place for a new dwelling, marking out its limits with a furrow; some make laws, establish judges and a sacred senate; some excavate a harbor; others lay the deep foundations for a theater; hewing tremendous pillars from the rocks, high decorations for the stage to come. They are like bees in early summer, busy in the sunlight . . . packing the cells with sweet nectar. . . . The work is fervent, and the fragrant honey is sweet with thyme.

Phoenicians made terra-cotta masks not to be worn by the living or even by the dead, but to be buried with the dead to repel evil spirits from the tomb. Archaeologists date this mask, excavated at Carthage, from 700 to 500 B.C.

World History Geography and History Activities **5**

Name _____ Date _____ Class _____

GEOGRAPHY and HISTORY Activity 3

Focus on Place

We normally think of a place in physical terms—where it is located and what landforms or structures it has. But the people who live in a place also define it. How many people are there? How fast is the population growing? Answers to these questions begin to identify the unique qualities of a place in human terms. When we discuss matters such as population size, change, density, or distribution, we are speaking in terms of human geography.

The population patterns of a place are frequently part of larger patterns that include events or conditions in other places. The flow of settlers across the Mediterranean from Tyre affected the Phoenician city-state as well as the "New City."

1. If you had to define a place without using physical terms, how would you do it? _____

2. What would you need to know in order to describe Carthage's population in geographic terms? _____

3. Describe the town or city where you live in terms of its human characteristics. _____

4. Characteristics such as income, age, and ethnic background also describe populations. Use one of these characteristics to describe a way that you are part of a national or global population.

Critical Thinking

5. **Making Inferences** Although Tyre gave up the practice of human sacrifice, the Carthaginians reintroduced it and became notorious for offering children to their cruel god, Baal. Why do you think that the peoples of Tyre and Carthage, despite their common roots, differed in their religious practices?

6. **Determining Cause and Effect** Over time the Carthaginians developed the rich farmlands near Carthage and began selling grain to other cities. How do you think this development changed population patterns in the Mediterranean?

Activity

7. The Phoenician word for the fort at Carthage, *boursa*, sounds similar to the Greek word *byrsa*, which means "oxhide." Some historians believe this word similarity is the basis of the oxhide legend. Using a place name as your basis, make up your own legend about the founding of a place.

GEOGRAPHY and HISTORY Activity 4

Location: *Lost Atlantis*

According to the Greek philosopher Plato, the deities 9,000 years earlier decided to punish the people of Atlantis for their wickedness. After a sudden catastrophe, Atlantis sank beneath the sea in a day and a night. Are legends of ancient Greece, such as Plato's story of Atlantis, rooted in actual geography?

In the 300s B.C., Plato recorded a story supposedly brought from Egypt about 200 years earlier by the Athenian statesman and poet Solon. According to Plato's account, Atlantis met its end about 9600 B.C.

Later, in the A.D. 1500s, when Europeans ventured across the Atlantic Ocean to explore the Americas, their voyages renewed interest in Plato's story and fueled speculation that Atlantis was a continent lost under the Atlantic Ocean or perhaps was even America. Many writers have since suggested that the Azores, Madeira, the Canaries, and the Cape Verde islands—in the eastern Atlantic—are in fact the mountaintops of a submerged continent.

Because Plato's detailed description of Atlantis matches well what archaeologists know of Bronze Age civilizations, it is unlikely that Atlantis flourished at a date earlier than the Neolithic Revolution. This discrepancy, along with other evidence, has suggested to some modern scholars that Plato or Solon was off by a factor of 10 in transcribing ancient Egyptian accounts. In other words, Atlantis was destroyed only about 900 years before Plato wrote, rather than 9,000 years earlier—that is, in prehistoric times. Plato may in fact have left us with a true historical account of the volcanic cataclysm known to have destroyed a great Minoan city on Thera, an island in the Aegean Sea about 70 miles (110 kilometers) north of Crete.

Plato's Account

But at a later time there occurred . . . earthquakes and floods, . . . and the island of Atlantis in like manner was swallowed up by the sea; wherefore also the ocean at that spot has now become impassable and unsearchable. . . .

And . . . [the sea god Poseidon] gave names, giving to him that was eldest and king the name after which the whole island was called and the sea spoken of as the Atlantic, because the first king who then reigned has the name of Atlas.

—from *Timaeus* and *Critias*, 300s. B.C.

Scientists' Theory

This suggested solution is not based on conjecture or myths but on a geological occurrence beyond challenge. . . . In the High Bronze Age around 1500 B.C. [as we interpret Plato's account] a dominant maritime power, Atlantis, threatening both Egypt and Athens, disappeared in a single day and night in a frightful natural cataclysm. Around 1500 B.C. a round island in the Aegean with no-known Minoan connections—Stronghyle-Santorin [Thera]—collapsed into the sea in a large volcanic eruption with side effects which caused such devastation to Minoan Crete . . . that [it] never recovered.

—from A.G. Galanopoulos and E. Bacon, *Atlantis: The Truth Behind the Legend*

Name _____ Date _____ Class _____

GEOGRAPHY and HISTORY Activity 4

Focus on Location

The location of places can be described using absolute or relative terms. Relative location can be given by compass directions or distances from other landmarks. To say that Greece is west of Turkey or that it borders on the Mediterranean Sea is to give a relative location, because the location of Greece is stated in terms of its relation to other landmarks in the area. Plato's account suggested that Atlantis may have been near the Pillars of Hercules, the ancient name of the Rock of Gibraltar.

1. What does "relative location" mean?

2. Using maps in your textbook, give the location of Greece relative to its position on the continent, proximity to water bodies, and surrounding countries.

3. Why does Plato's mention of Atlantis's war with both Athens and Egypt suggest the relative location of Atlantis?

4. What features of Atlantis might identify it as a Bronze Age civilization rather than a pre-Neolithic society?

Critical Thinking

5. **Synthesizing Information** To the Egyptians of about 1500 B.C., the islands of Crete and Thera (about 400 and 480 miles, or 640 and 770 kilometers, from Egypt) seemed very far away. Why has people's perception of "far away" changed over the years?

6. **Drawing Conclusions** According to Greek mythology, Atlas supported the pillars that held heaven and earth apart; the name Atlantic Ocean means "Sea of Atlas." Why do you think the Atlantic Ocean got this name?

Activity

7. Select a well-known place in your local area, then ask five people to describe its location. On a separate sheet of paper, compare these descriptions. Did everyone give the same relative location?

8   Geography and History Activities   World History

GEOGRAPHY and HISTORY Activity 5

Region: *The Greek Language*

Archaeologists excavating a site near Ai Khanum in northern Afghanistan found a stone slab bearing Greek inscriptions. They also found a papyrus written in Greek discussing Aristotelian philosophy. How did the Greek language spread so far?

The Greek artifacts excavated near Ai Khanum are the remains of a remote outpost of the Greco-Bactrian Kingdom, which was once part of Alexander the Great's empire. About 200 B.C., people from the Greco-Bactrian Kingdom would have been able to speak with people in Egypt, Syria, Asia Minor, and even Spain—because they all spoke Koine (koy • NAY), a dialect of the Greek language.

In the early years of the Hellenistic era—the late 300s B.C.—the everyday language for many of the people conquered by Alexander was Aramic or Persian, but the Greeks and Macedonians, who settled in the cities throughout Alexander's empire, spoke Greek. The Greek language first came to be used by political administrators, judges, and scholars, but merchants and travelers quickly adopted it as well. A new, streamlined version of Greek emerged in the Hellenistic cities and was called the *koine dialektos*, or "common language."

Gradually Koine became commonly spoken throughout the Hellenistic world. In about 250 B.C., Jewish scholars in Alexandria, Egypt, translated Hebrew scriptures into Koine. The Apostle Paul, in the first century A.D., wrote his letters to fellow Christians in Koine, and even those portions of the New Testament written in Aramic were quickly translated into Koine.

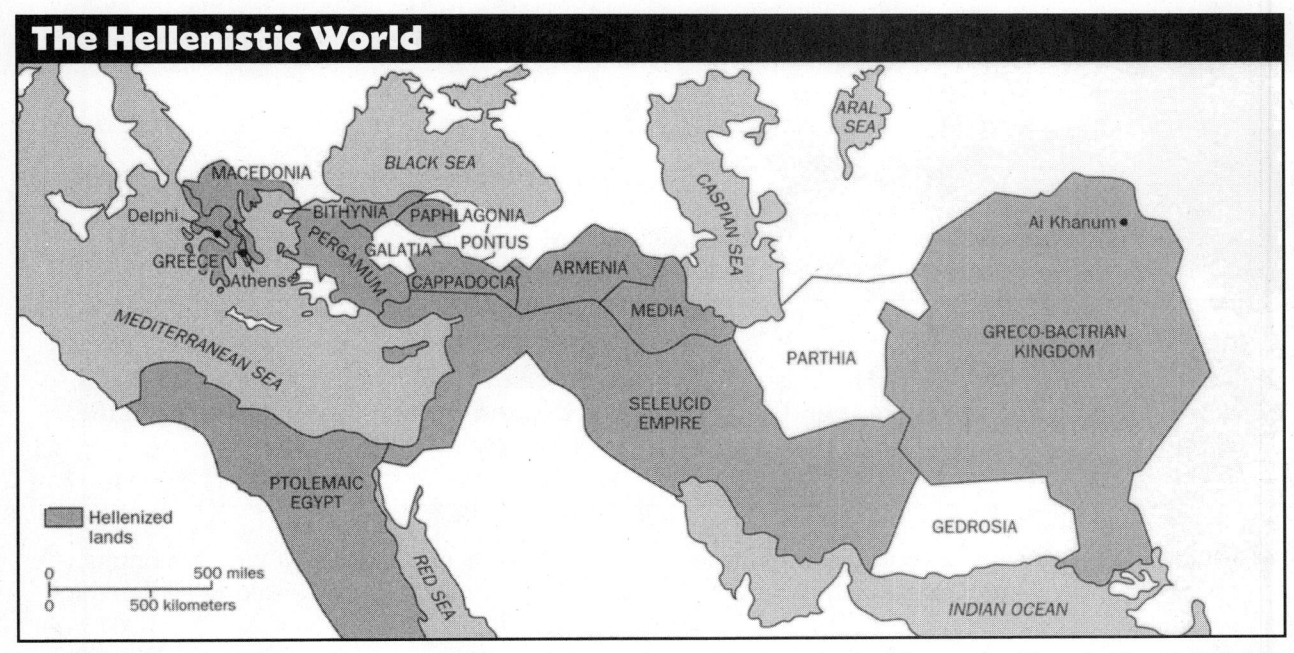

The Hellenistic World

Macedonia became a world power under Alexander the Great, who extended his empire as far as India. Alexander founded 70 cities that continued as cultural centers long after his empire faded away.

Name _____ Date _____ Class _____

GEOGRAPHY and HISTORY Activity 5

Focus on Region

Regions are the basic units that geographers use to study the range of people and places around the world. By determining which places share a common characteristic—such as climate, vegetation, culture, language, or political structure—geographers can define specific regions. After regions have been defined, geographers can simplify and organize information about places into manageable chunks and thus make the task of analyzing geographic information easier.

Defining the Hellenistic world as a cultural region helps you understand ancient history. The boundaries are defined by what were the cultural characteristics of the region for a particular historical time. The common use of the Greek Koine unified the Hellenistic world for more than three centuries, well into Roman times.

1. Why do geographers divide the world into regions?
_____

2. Why wouldn't political divisions for 185 B.C. define the Hellenistic world as a single region?
_____
_____

3. What else besides the use of Greek in what is now Afghanistan do the Ai Khanum archaeological finds suggest?
_____
_____

4. Use the map scale to determine the distance between Ai Khanum and the Greek mainland.
_____

Critical Thinking

5. **Analyzing Information** The Hellenistic world can also be defined as a region based on its economic features. How were trade and commerce related to the spread of Koine throughout the region?
_____

6. **Making Comparisons** Language can be used to define regions today. In what way are English-speaking America and Spanish-speaking America equivalent to the Koine-speaking Hellenistic world?
_____

Activity

7. Compare the map of the Hellenistic world with a variety of maps of the area today—physical, vegetation, climate, religion, and others. How could you best define modern regional boundaries for the geographic area that once was the Hellenistic region?

Name .... Date .... Class ....

GEOGRAPHY and HISTORY Activity 6

Movement: *Roman Roads*

People in the modern city of Rome still drive over portions of the Appian Way. Started in 312 B.C. by Appius Claudius Caecus, the Appian Way was one of the first Roman military highways. How did the Roman Empire use its roads?

Ever since draft animals first pulled wheeled vehicles, people have built roads, and the best road builders of the ancient world were the Romans. Road building was a key factor in Roman military conquest, enabling generals to move their legions quickly from one flash point to another in a vast empire. Roman soldiers could cover 30 miles (48 kilometers) a day if roads were firm and dry. Eventually a network of more than 50,000 miles (80,000 kilometers) of roads, regularly marked with milestones, laced together the Roman Empire.

Designed to handle military carts hauling cargo weighing as much as 1,000 Roman pounds (330 kilograms), Roman roads have lasted for centuries. While earlier roads often meandered along animal trails and contours of the terrain, Roman roads cut a remarkably straight line no matter what obstacles lay in their path—swamps, mountains, and even ravines.

Construction began with engineers laying out two trenches 40 feet (12 meters) apart, enabling them to analyze the composition of the subsoil. Then under the watchful eyes of supervisors, teams of soldiers dug down several feet to prepare the roadbed. On top of the flattened layer of sand came three additional layers that cushioned the top layer of paving stones.

A convex road surface—sloped from the center down toward the sides—drained water off the road into ditches. In almost any weather, legions of troops, merchants with carts, and postal carriages could continue their journeys. Most private individuals rode two-wheeled chariots behind a team of two to four horses. The fastest four-wheeled freight wagons were drawn by eight horses in summer and ten during the winter. They sped past most traffic, covering up to 75 miles (120 kilometers) per day.

The Appian Way

[Appius Claudius Caecus] caused all the paving stones to be polished and cut so as to form angles and had them jointed together without any kind of cement. They adhered so strongly that to look at them they do not seem to be jointed at all but to form one whole mosaic of stone.

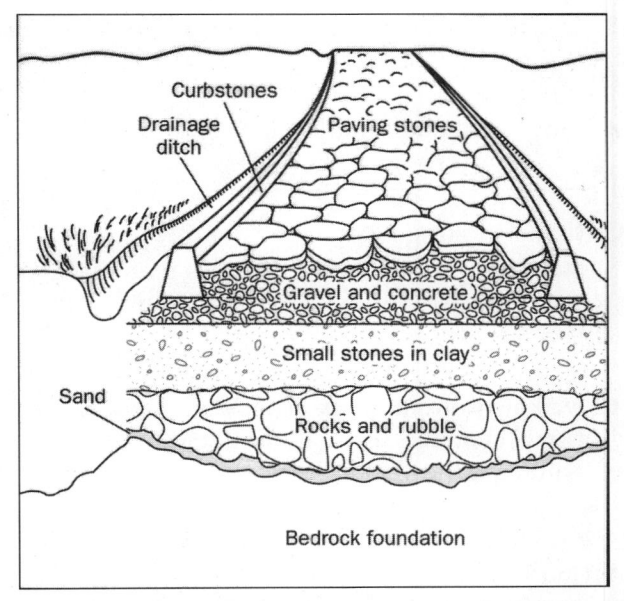

The Romans adapted their road-building technology to the terrain and also to available building materials. The road shown would have been constructed on solid dry ground. In an unstable, marshy area, the Romans would have laid a road on timber foundations pinned to the ground by stakes.

World History — Geography and History Activities — 11

Name .... Date .... Class ....

GEOGRAPHY and HISTORY Activity 6

Focus on Movement

People in different places and at different times have developed a variety of ways to move over distances—by land and by sea and, most recently, by air. These methods of travel have been used to carry people, their natural resources, their manufactured goods, and even their ideas. Over the years, the movement of people develops a regular pattern, in some places following the same major historical trade routes for many centuries. In other places people may carve out new routes of travel. To develop economically and politically, people must create an effective transportation network to link all parts of their territory. In addition, they can improve their means of transportation with technological innovations—for example, in the areas of navigation, shipbuilding, road building, and laying railroad tracks.

1. What sorts of things do people need to be able to move?
   _____

2. Why did a system of roads help the Romans develop economically and politically?
   _____

3. List three adjectives or phrases to describe Roman roads.
   _____

4. How was road building militarily important to the Romans?
   _____

Critical Thinking

5. **Analyzing Information** Rome's roads facilitated administering a vast empire. What is the meaning of the expression "all roads lead to Rome"?
   _____

6. **Making Comparisons** The "highways" of the ancient Greeks were actually sea-lanes and navigational channels throughout the Mediterranean Sea. Compare the advantages of movement by water for the Greeks with movement by land for the Romans.
   _____

Activity

7. Modern roads are designed by highly trained civil engineers. Write an essay explaining the ways modern roads are similar to ancient Roman roads and ways they are different. What problems might a civil engineer face in designing roads today?

12 Geography and History Activities   World History

GEOGRAPHY and HISTORY Activity 7

Place: *The Discovery of Jenne-jeno*

Artifacts from the first archaeological dig at Jenne-jeno raised many questions. When archaeologists Susan and Roderick McIntosh returned to Mali in 1981, they hoped to unearth more remains that would prove Jenne-jeno was the oldest city in West Africa. Why do you think that this once thriving city was abandoned in about A.D. 1400?

After a month of labor in the hot sun and fierce winds of the Niger River, the McIntoshes' 1981 excavation unlocked some of the mysteries of how Jenne-jeno had changed over hundreds of years. The oldest artifacts indicated that the people living there around 275 B.C. fished, herded animals, and lived in circular houses.

But the most remarkable finds were the remains of workshops for making copper and iron utensils, since the nearest deposits of iron ore and copper were 31 miles (50 kilometers) away. The metal artifacts dated 400 years before the arrival of Islamic traders in West Africa.

Finding West Africa's Oldest City

Our luck far exceeded expectations. Each of the four pits we dug yielded abundant evidence.... Animal bones, rice chaff, and carbonized grains documented a mixed diet. Pottery fragments, spindle whorls, terra-cotta statuary, and crucibles for smelting copper or gold gave insight into local arts and crafts. Walls defined sturdy homes.
—Susan and Roderick McIntosh, in an account of their 1981 dig

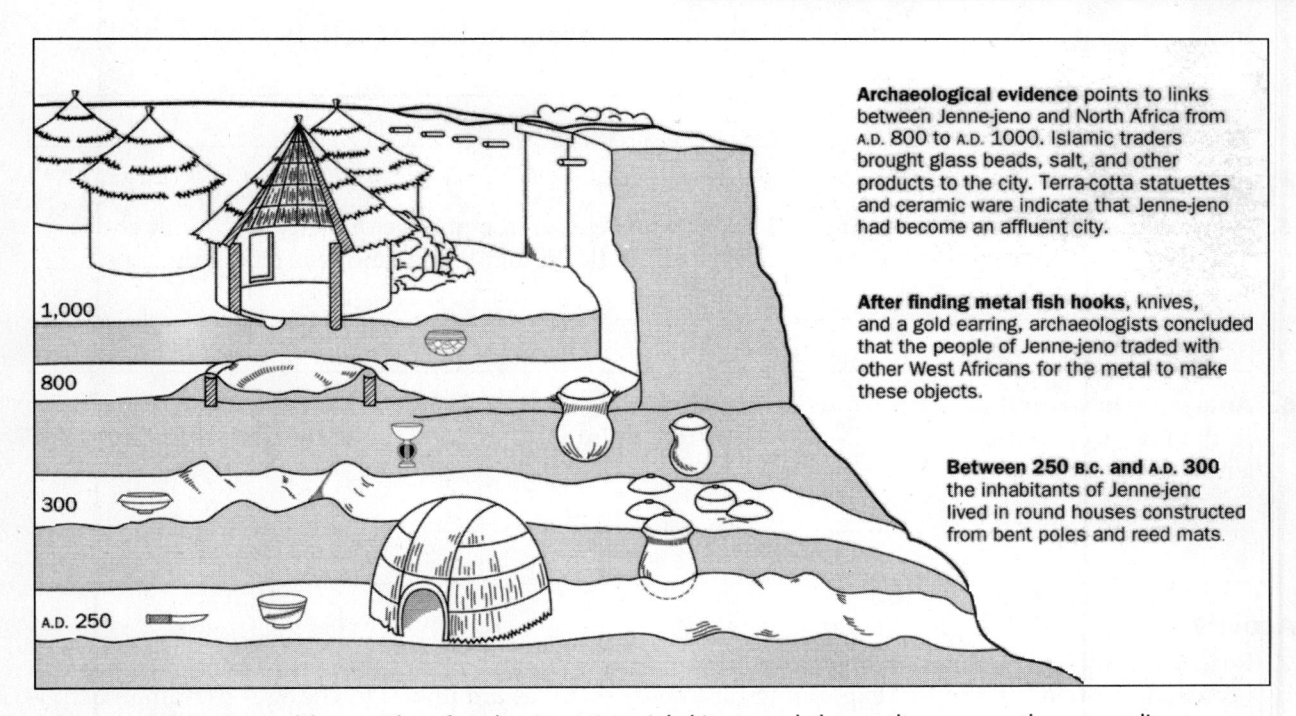

Archaeological evidence points to links between Jenne-jeno and North Africa from A.D. 800 to A.D. 1000. Islamic traders brought glass beads, salt, and other products to the city. Terra-cotta statuettes and ceramic ware indicate that Jenne-jeno had become an affluent city.

After finding metal fish hooks, knives, and a gold earring, archaeologists concluded that the people of Jenne-jeno traded with other West Africans for the metal to make these objects.

Between 250 B.C. and A.D. 300 the inhabitants of Jenne-jeno lived in round houses constructed from bent poles and reed mats.

A pattern of trade emerged from artifacts found at Jenne-jeno. Inhabitants traded crops they grew on the surrounding floodplain for metal to make knives, spears, and fishhooks.

Name _____ Date _____ Class _____

GEOGRAPHY and HISTORY Activity 7

Focus on Place

People develop land for many uses—for houses, factories, public buildings, and recreation. Patterns of land use emerge and then change as development continues. Whether land is used for highways, industrial parks, or conservation areas, its use reflects the needs and values of the inhabitants of a place.

By looking at the artifacts that people left many years ago, the McIntoshes were able to reconstruct a picture of the physical characteristics of Jenne-jeno and its cultural life. They studied the customs of people living in the modern city of Jenne and found links to the social and commercial life of the people of Jenne-jeno.

1. How do human actions affect the character of a place over time?

2. Which artifacts indicate that people in Jenne-jeno lived near a river?

3. What conclusions can you draw from the presence of glass beads at the Jenne-jeno site around A.D. 1000?

4. In what way do you think trade might have led to continuing changes in Jenne-jeno?

Critical Thinking

5. **Demonstrating Reasoned Judgment** The McIntoshes found evidence of a city wall built about A.D. 1000. How would the evidence of a city wall indicate that Jenne-jeno was changing?

6. **Analyzing Information** Archaeologists piece together a story about a place from the artifacts they find. How do you think the terra-cotta statuettes fit into the cultural life of the people of Jenne-jeno?

Activity

7. Research how land use has changed in your community. Use maps to show the changes that have occurred. Write a brief report explaining how these changes are linked to changes in human activities in your community or region.

Name .... Date .... Class ....

GEOGRAPHY and HISTORY Activity 8

Place: *Monsoons of India*

Across the arid plains of northern India, hot dry winds send grit and dust flying, blackening the sky. Soon the monsoon will arrive. Until then, tension is high as the temperature and the winds continue to rise. How does the extreme nature of the monsoons affect India?

Monsoons are seasonal winds that change direction twice a year. The word *monsoon* is derived from the Arabic *mausim*, meaning "season." In Asia a summer, or southwest, monsoon blows from mid-May through September and brings heavy rains from tropical oceans. A winter, or northeast, monsoon is a wind in the reverse direction, which begins during October and brings cool, dry, continental air.

For rural India, the arrival of the monsoon signifies the renewal of life. The monsoon can mean survival itself for farmers, since half of India's arable land depends solely on monsoon rains and a single growing season. When the monsoon is delayed, drought and famine can affect millions of people. Food prices then soar, causing inflation. Urban life can also be complicated by a delay in the arrival of the monsoon. About half of India's electricity is generated by hydropower and thus by the monsoons. While the monsoon can sometimes skip entire regions, a particularly harsh downpour can bring cyclones and floods to low-lying coastlines.

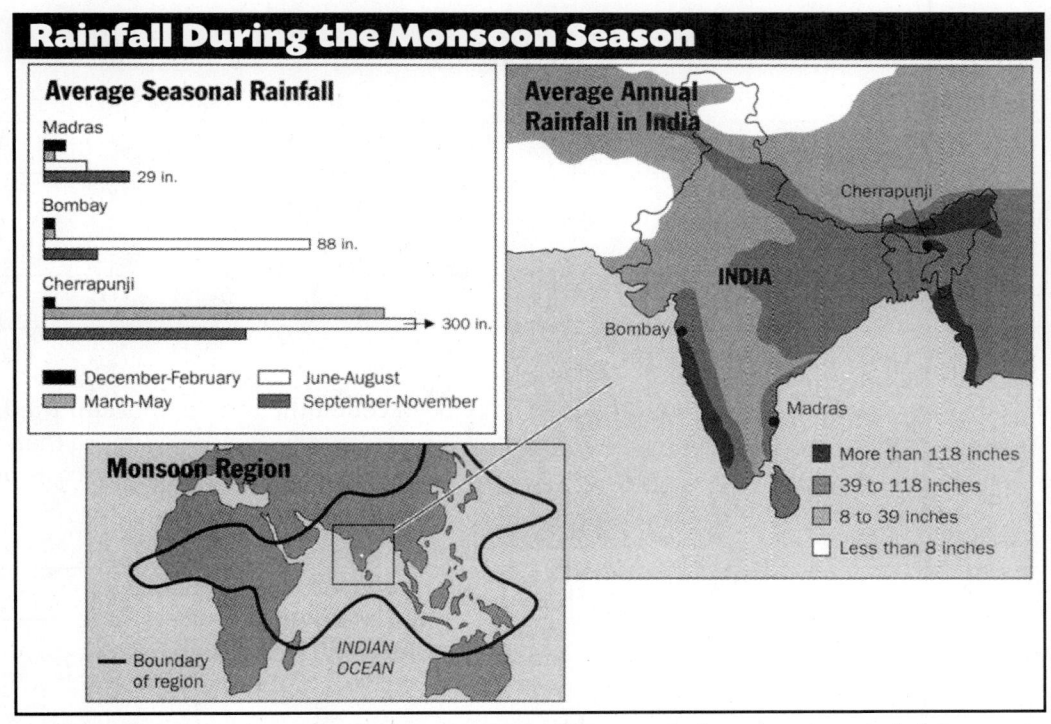

Rainfall During the Monsoon Season

Average Seasonal Rainfall
- Madras: 29 in.
- Bombay: 88 in.
- Cherrapunji: 300 in.

Legend: December–February, June–August, March–May, September–November

Average Annual Rainfall in India
- More than 118 inches
- 39 to 118 inches
- 8 to 39 inches
- Less than 8 inches

Cities shown: Bombay, Madras, Cherrapunji

Monsoon Region — Boundary of region, Indian Ocean

Asian agriculture and the survival of half the world's 5.5 billion people depend on the arrival of the monsoon, one of the most massive—and unpredictable—weather systems in the world. Late rains can have far-reaching economic, political, and social consequences in India.

World History   Geography and History Activities

Name .... Date .... Class ....

GEOGRAPHY and HISTORY Activity 8

Focus on Place

You can describe a place by its physical and human characteristics. Physical characteristics include climate, landforms, water forms, vegetation, and animal life. Monsoons are a distinguishing physical characteristic of India. A cycle of air set in motion by temperature differences over land and sea produces the monsoon season, which in turn affects other aspects of the nation's physical environment. Erosion of land, for example, is a significant result of monsoons, in which topsoil is washed away to sea. Exposed earth, especially in the mountains, cannot withstand the downpours of the monsoon, leading to devastation of the physical environment with dangerous landslides and loss of vegetation.

1. What are some physical characteristics that describe a place?

2. Describe India's monsoon season.

3. How would a delay in the arrival of the monsoon affect rural and urban Indians?

4. What aspects of Indian life are affected by the climate?

Critical Thinking

5. **Predicting Consequences** Monsoon forecasts have been called the most important predictions in the world, yet the onset of the monsoon rains cannot be accurately predicted more than a few days in advance. Why are these forecasts so crucial? How do you think these forecasts affect people in India?

6. **Making Inferences** Why would Indians perceive rain and clouds differently from people in the West?

Activity

7. With your classmates, brainstorm a list of seasonal changes in climate in the United States. How do these changes affect physical and human environments in different parts of the country during the year?

Name .... Date .... Class ....

GEOGRAPHY and HISTORY Activity 9

Region: *The Silk Road*

In the first two centuries A.D., a silken thread linked the two greatest empires—the Roman Empire and the Han Empire. From Rome to Changan, the Silk Road stretched some 7,000 miles. How did trade take place over this longest road in the world?

Few merchants ever made the complete journey from one end of the Silk Road to the other. Instead, they traveled along shorter segments, winding through tranquil empires as well as regions at war for precious goods that had crossed deserts and mountains. By means of this trade among regions, the pampered nobility of Rome obtained translucent silks, and China's highborn acquired Roman gold, silver, amber, colored glass, and wool.

A thousand years later, from 1271 to 1275, the Venetian merchant Marco Polo traveled the Silk Road in its entirety. The Silk Road continues to connect cultures today, although most travelers use it for shorter stretches, like the journeys of long ago.

The Travels of Marco Polo

At the extremity of the plain . . . there is a descent for about twenty miles, by a road that is extremely dangerous, from the multitude of robbers by whom travellers are continually assaulted and plundered. At length you reach . . . a city named Hormuz, a port frequented by traders . . . who bring spices and medicines, precious stones, pearls, gold tissues, elephants' teeth, and various other articles of merchandise. These they dispose of to a different set of traders, by whom they are dispersed throughout the world.

—Marco Polo's account of his journey to China, 1298

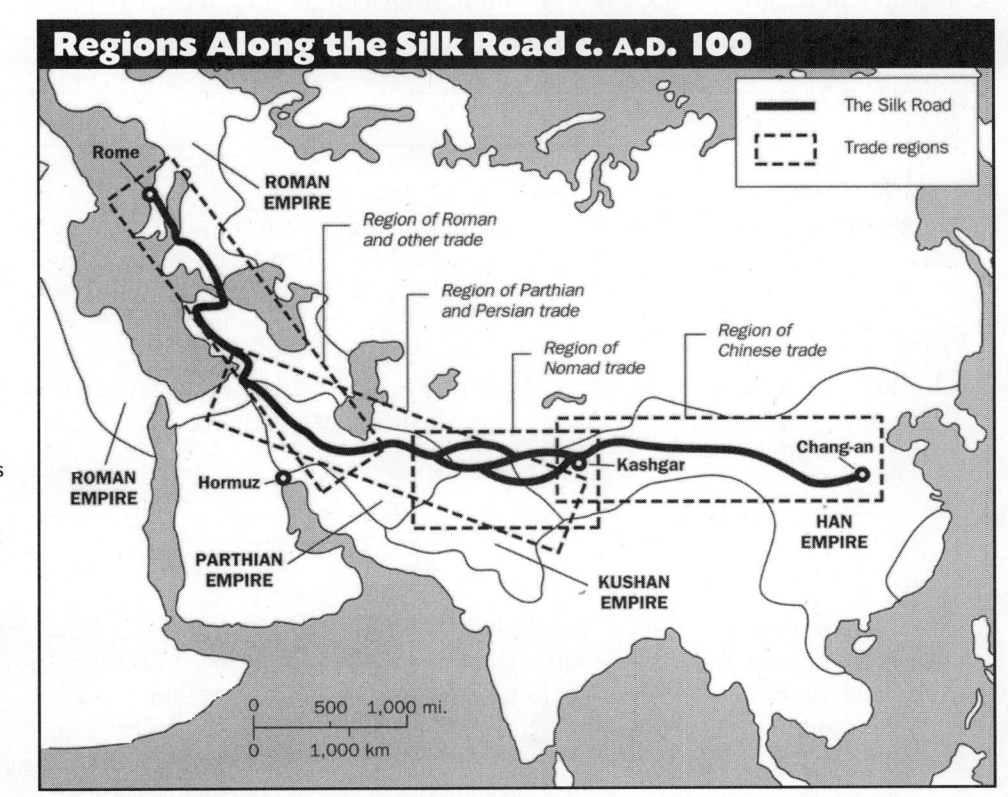

Regions Along the Silk Road c. A.D. 100

Exchanges among merchants of different lands created trade regions. Generally, Roman, Greek, and Arab merchants passed their goods on to Persians and nomads from central Asia. The Persians then traded those items for silk, furs, rhubarb, and cinnamon in exchanges with Chinese merchants near Kashgar.

World History   Geography and History Activities   **17**

Name .... Date .... Class ....

GEOGRAPHY and HISTORY Activity 9

Focus on Region

Because a region is simply an area that has one or more common characteristics, many different types and sizes of regions may be defined within a single larger area. It all depends on your criteria—the reasons you choose to define a region. As criteria change, the boundaries of regions also change.

If you want to define important language regions along the Silk Road, for example, one region you will identify is the area where Indo-European languages were spoken. Its boundaries overlap boundaries between empires and trading regions. Knowing that Persian, nomadic, and Roman traders had similar languages can help explain why they roamed far along the Silk Road, whereas traders speaking Chinese stayed close to home.

1. What is a region?

2. How can one place be in several different regions?

3. How does examining the boundaries of a language region help you understand trade regions along the Silk Road?

4. What error about regions would result if you assumed that merchants traded only within the boundaries of their own empires?

Critical Thinking

5. **Determining Cause and Effect** Sometime during the first few centuries A.D., Westerners smuggled silkworms out of China. What effect do you think this had on trade along the Silk Road?

6. **Checking Consistency** If you were to draw boundaries of mountain chains onto the map of the Silk Road, would you expect them to be the same as or different from the boundaries of political regions (empires)? Why?

Activity

7. The Chinese received millions of dollars' worth of gold and silver in trade for silk each year. Some historians believe that this unequal trade weakened the Roman Empire. Regarding present-day trade, debate the following question: Will trade with Asia weaken the West?

GEOGRAPHY and HISTORY Activity 10

Place: *Constantinople*

"One could not believe there was so rich a city in all the world," noted the crusader Villehardouin about the splendor of Constantinople. In its glory from the A.D. 500s to 1000s, this "New Rome" on the Bosporus was dedicated to the Christian religion. What role did Constantinople play in the history of the Byzantine Empire?

The city of Constantinople, a center of trade and education, stood at the crossroads of Europe and Asia. Its citizens were the descendants of various peoples but still considered themselves Romans. Social acceptance depended on knowledge of the Greek language and adherence to the Christian faith. In preserving its Greek and Roman heritage, Constantinople also developed its own distinct culture.

A city of great power and pageantry, Constantinople was home to half a million people. Vessels that crowded its great harbor filled the city's markets with silks, spices, furs, precious stones, perfumed woods, carved ivory, gold and silver, and enameled jewelry. Within the walls of the fortress city stood magnificent examples of Byzantine architecture, such as the Hippodrome, the Great Palace, and the church of Hagia Sophia.

Life in Constantinople included government regulation of trade and industry, as well as control of banking, insurance, and credit services. The poor were put to work in state bakeries and market gardens. The lives of all citizens were also greatly affected by the close ties between the church and the state.

The Conquest of Constantinople

Indeed you should know that they gazed well at Constantinople, those who had never seen it; for they could not believe that there could be in all the world a city so rich, when they saw all those tall ramparts and the mighty towers with which it was shut all around, and those rich palaces and those tall churches, of which there were so many that nobody could believe their eyes, had they not seen it, and the length and breadth of the city which was sovereign among all others.

—Villehardouin

The significance of religion in Byzantine culture and the close ties between church and state are depicted in this mosaic. Emperor Constantine IX is shown holding a purse of money; his wife, Zoe, is holding a signed and sealed document confirming the donation to the Church, with Christ shown as the recipient.

World History — Geography and History Activities 19

Name .... Date .... Class ....

GEOGRAPHY and HISTORY
Activity 10

Focus on Place

You can describe a place by naming various physical and human characteristics that give an area its identity. Human characteristics include aspects of a culture—language, religion, political systems, economic activities, and social structures, for instance. Religion was a distinguishing human characteristic in the Byzantine capital of Constantinople (the present-day city of Istanbul, Turkey). The Christian religion influenced virtually every aspect of life, including art, architecture, and politics. By comparing the human characteristics of a place, such as the economic and religious activities of its people, you can determine significant features of each.

1. What are the human characteristics of a place?

2. Describe Constantinople's human characteristics.

3. What aspects of life in Constantinople were influenced by the Christian religion?

4. What human characteristics make your community distinct from other communities?

Critical Thinking

5. **Making Comparisons** Close ties existed between church and state in the Byzantine Empire. Compare that relationship to the relationship between church and state in the United States today.

6. **Drawing Conclusions** How might the human characteristics of a place affect its relations with other countries?

Activity

7. Read a local daily newspaper for one week, noting specific examples of how human characteristics influence or affect community life. At the end of the week, compile a list of the issues that reflect these human characteristics. Share your findings in a classroom discussion.

Geography and History Activity 11

Human-Environment Interaction: *Bedouin Life*

"Watering camels is hard work. They are thirsty and drink a lot, and the sun is hot. It is worse when the wind blows; then it is like a furnace. . . . Only the Bedu could endure this life," noted Wilfred Thesiger, an English explorer who crossed the Arabian Desert during the 1940s. Across the arid desert of the Middle East these nomads traveled, searching for fresh water and pastureland for their camels, goats, and sheep. How did the bedouin survive such harsh conditions?

Searing heat and scant rainfall meant a life of hardship for the desert nomad. For thousands of years, the bedouin have moved between pasture and oasis. Members of the same clan tent together near oases during the dry season, moving their herds out to desert pastures when the winter rains come. A close-knit society based on tribal loyalties and alliances has ensured survival. Traditionally, the bedouin have claimed certain grazing lands as *dirah*, or tribal territory. Tribe members continually fought to protect their lands and herds from raiding parties of other tribes. Marriage perpetuated divisions, as no member of a noble tribe would marry someone from a tribe of lesser status.

The bonds of tradition and loyalty that once made survival in the desert possible have been affected by recent changes in Arab society. The vast desert that was once crossed only by camels now bears a network of roads. The bedouin use trucks to travel from place to place, taking their families, their belongings, and their animals with them. Instead of herding animals from grazing spots to water holes, they now haul water to the animals by truck. The bedouin maintain their fierce independence, however, and continue their nomadic life.

> **Bedouin Proverb**
>
> *Me and my brother against our cousin.*
> *Me, my brother, and my cousin against the stranger.*

Modernization and new sources of wealth have brought changes to bedouin Arab life. Their Islamic culture, however, remains centered on hospitality, tribal courtesy, and family relationships.

GEOGRAPHY and HISTORY Activity 11

Focus on Human-Environment Interaction

People adapt to their physical environment in different ways. The areas in which they settle, the crops they grow, how they use resources, and how they respond culturally to their surroundings reflect this process of adaptation. The bedouin developed a migratory life to find water and pastureland for their animals. They established a pattern of trade with oasis settlements, exchanging animal skins and meat for such goods as clothing and the fruit of the date palm. The harsh life of desert nomads on the Arabian Peninsula has affected other aspects of bedouin culture. Competition among tribes for limited resources such as wells and grazing areas results in raiding and blood feuds, further shaping bedouin values, customs, and loyalties.

1. How does physical environment affect peoples' lives?

2. Why is adaptation to physical environment necessary?

3. What are some examples of adaptation to physical environment?

4. Why would family ties be so important to the bedouin?

Critical Thinking

5. **Making Comparisons** Compare the ways in which members of Byzantine society adapted to their physical environment with the ways in which the bedouin adapted to their surroundings.

6. **Synthesizing Information** On a separate sheet of paper, write a short paragraph describing the ways in which people in your community have adapted culturally to their surroundings.

Activity

7. Research how the lives of the bedouin have changed since World War II and write a short report. In your report, address the following question: Since World War II, how have Arab governments sought to integrate the bedouin into modern Arab society? Have these methods met with success? Why or why not?

Name .... Date .... Class ....

GEOGRAPHY and HISTORY Activity 12

Movement: *Vikings*

Off the Northumbrian coast of northeastern Britain sped long, low ships with high, curving prows and sterns. The ships rammed onto the undefended beaches of Lindisfarne—a lonely and windswept island, home only to the monks of St. Cuthbert's monastery. Fearsome, screaming warriors poured from the bellies of these great sailing vessels. What were the invaders seeking?

The warriors who attacked and raided St. Cuthbert's in A.D. 793 were skilled sailors, fierce fighters, and greedy looters. They wreaked havoc as they hacked their way into the monastery's chapels and storerooms, looking for jewel-covered illuminated manuscripts, golden crucifixes, and silver communion vessels. Bloody raids followed in Britain and Ireland and, by the A.D. 840s, in France as well. So many churches and monasteries were robbed that a new prayer was added to the Christian litany: "From the fury of the Northmen, O Lord, deliver us."

Known as the Vikings, these fighting men—Scandinavians from Norway, Denmark, and Sweden—sought new sources of land, fame, and wealth. Vikings were attracted to areas throughout eastern and western Europe that offered luxury items such as gold and silver; a Nordic warrior's success in life was measured by his plunder. Vikings often buried their treasures. The contents of such hoards reflect Viking movement during the A.D. 800s and 900s. Nordic traders who traveled into Russia and met Arab traders, for instance, buried silver that had originated from the coinage of the caliphate. Other hidden Viking treasures came from silver deposits that originated in Germany.

Siege of Paris

The town trembles, and horns resound, the walls are bathed in floods of tears, the whole region laments: from the river are heard the horn blasts. Stones and spears one on top of another fly through the air. Our men give a loud battle cry which is answered by the Danes. Suddenly the earth shakes (as a tower falls): our men lament, the Danes rejoice. Reinforcements fighting bravely try to reach those groaning in the tower; but in vain.

—Abbon's account of attack in A.D. 886

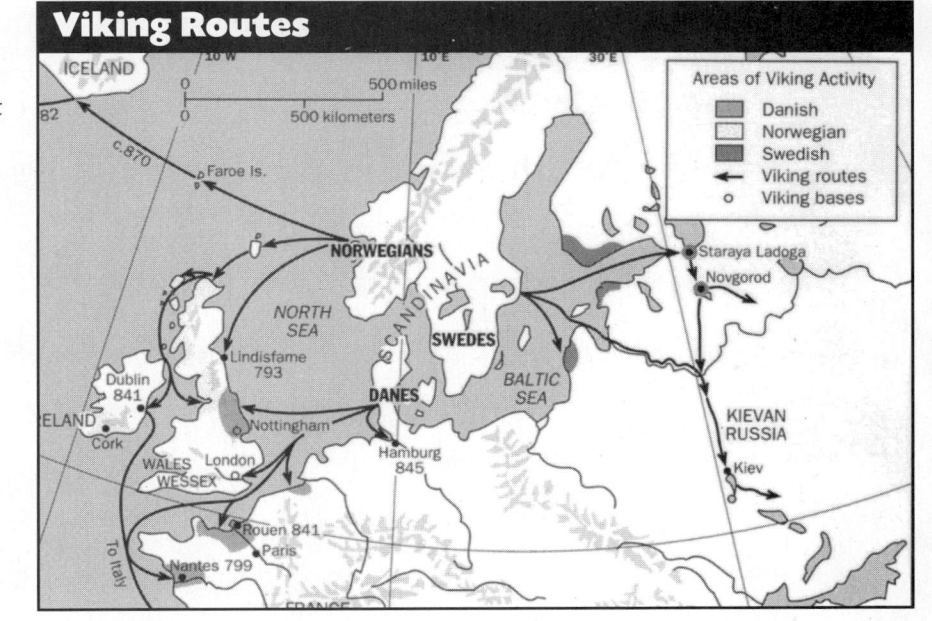

Viking activity in western Europe during the A.D. 800s reflected the warriors' interest in attaining wealth, status, and fame.

World History

Geography and History Activities **23**

Name _____ Date _____ Class _____

GEOGRAPHY and HISTORY Activity 12

Focus on Movement

Few places in the world are entirely self-sufficient. Resources are often distributed unequally among areas and people. At times people move to new locations in order to meet their needs; at other times trade enables resources and products to be more equally distributed. Viking movement in Europe initially focused on trading and raiding. Over time, however, the Vikings changed their activities, from trading and raiding to conquest and settlement. Patterns of Viking movement—whether by trade, warfare, or settlement—established new networks of transportation and communication.

1. Explain how the needs of certain groups can affect their movement.
   _____

2. Which factors influenced Viking movement?
   _____

3. What are other examples of movement that resulted in new networks of transportation and communication?
   _____
   _____

4. Why do you think the Vikings traded with the Europeans and then turned to conquest and settlement?
   _____
   _____

Critical Thinking

5. **Drawing Conclusions** What do buried Viking treasures tell us about the Scandinavian warriors?
   _____
   _____

6. **Identifying Alternatives** How could Europeans have defended themselves against the Vikings?
   _____
   _____

Activity

7. Organize a debate on the following topic: The Vikings sailed to North America before Christopher Columbus.

Name .... Date .... Class ....

GEOGRAPHY and HISTORY Activity 13

Human-Environment Interaction: *Gothic Cathedrals*

"Whether lifting our eyes to the soaring nave vaults, or peering into the depths of the aisles, the whole atmosphere is one of religious mystery. . . . [One] cannot but experience a little of that unearthly joy so keenly felt by the devotees of our cathedral." What impression do these words by Etienne Houvet, curator of Chartres, give of this French cathedral?

Reflecting the central role of the Church in people's lives during the Middle Ages, cathedrals were built for the glory of God. During the A.D. 1100s, a new system of construction that originated in France signaled a change in architectural style from Roman to Gothic. The Gothic style of architecture would allow people to achieve new heights in honoring God.

A fine example of Gothic architecture, Our Lady of Chartres was rebuilt following a fire in A.D. 1194. The new structure, with a vault that reaches 11 stories into the sky, attests to the success of medieval builders in devising new ways to distribute the weight of cathedral walls. Ribbed vaults, pointed arches, and flying buttresses allowed stained-glass windows to fill the interior with light and the walls to stretch to the heavens.

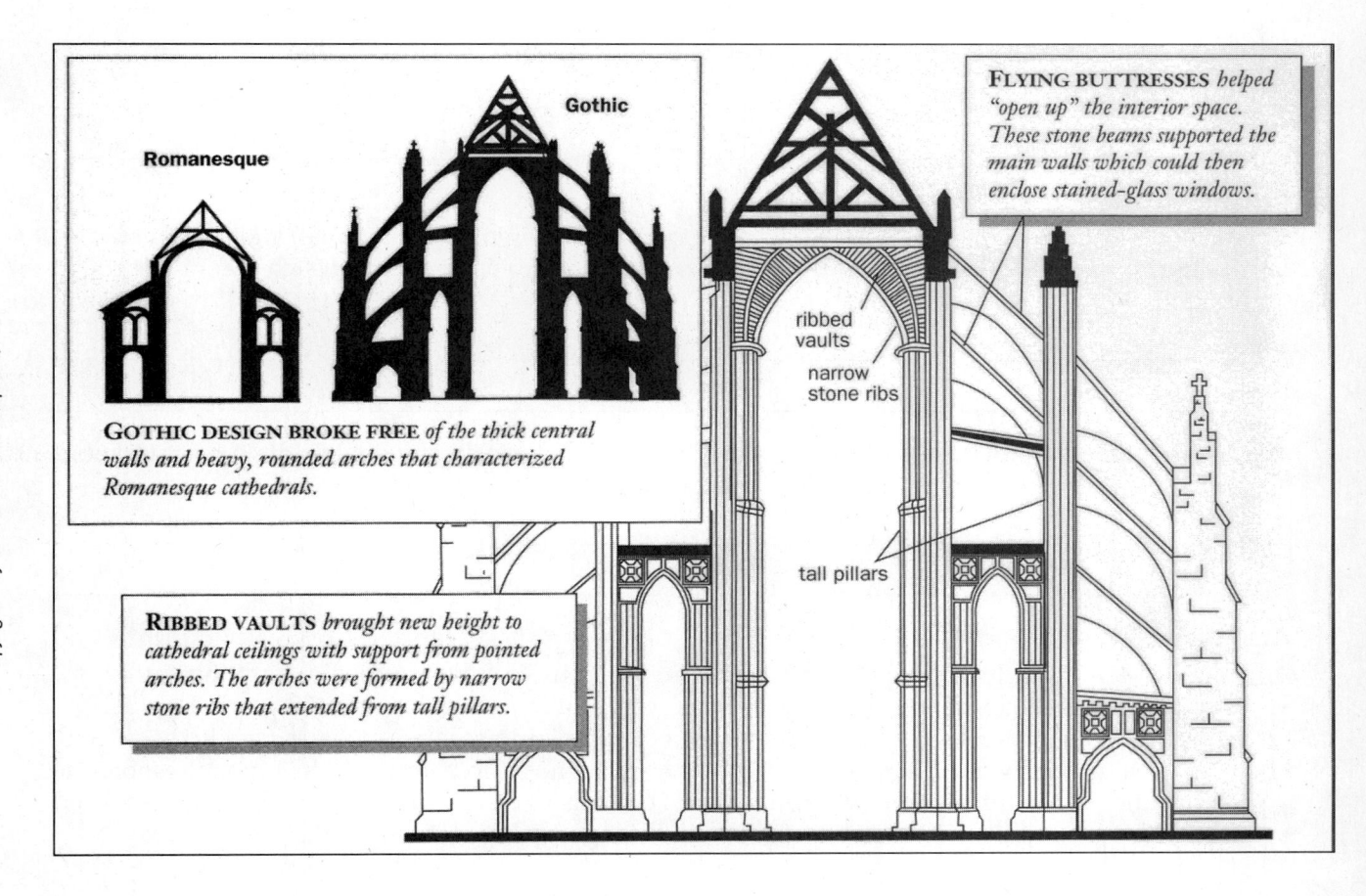

GOTHIC DESIGN BROKE FREE of the thick central walls and heavy, rounded arches that characterized Romanesque cathedrals.

RIBBED VAULTS brought new height to cathedral ceilings with support from pointed arches. The arches were formed by narrow stone ribs that extended from tall pillars.

FLYING BUTTRESSES helped "open up" the interior space. These stone beams supported the main walls which could then enclose stained-glass windows.

World History   Geography and History Activities   **25**

Name .... Date .... Class ....

GEOGRAPHY and HISTORY Activity 13

Focus on Human-Environment Interaction

People's ability to modify their surroundings has grown as they have improved their technology. Improvements have been made in tools, transportation, and materials. Gothic cathedrals represent an improvement in design discovered during the Middle Ages. This architectural innovation revolutionized construction and focused the energies of towns and entire regions. Stonemasons, architects, and other skilled workers contributed to this innovation.

1. How can people's use of technology affect their ability to modify their physical environments?

2. Describe how this ability has increased through the use of technology.

3. Give examples of how architecture and engineering have modified physical environments.

4. Are there any developing technologies that may affect your physical environment? Explain.

Critical Thinking

5. Making Inferences Medieval cathedrals were centers of religious, educational, and social activities during the Middle Ages. Why do you think it was so important to have such magnificent buildings?

6. Making Comparisons Compare changes in architectural styles during the Middle Ages with more recent examples of people's modification of their physical environments.

Activity

7. To understand how technology can be used to modify physical environments, form three groups to conduct research on physical changes in your community during the past 50 years. The first group will read local newspapers to determine how new technologies were described. The second group will interview members of their families and neighbors to determine the human response to modifications. The third group will contact local officials to discuss how technology has been used to alter the community's physical environment. Each group should present its findings to the class.

Name _____ Date _____ Class _____

GEOGRAPHY and HISTORY Activity 14

Location: *Strait of Malacca*

At a busy wharf on the island of Sumatra in the A.D. 1300s, an Islamic trader bends over bags of aromatic spices—cloves, nutmeg, and mace. Stacks of sandalwood and bolts of silk are piled nearby. A local agent bargains with Indian and Chinese traders. What mainland kingdoms existed in Southeast Asia at about this time?

For hundreds of years, the Strait of Malacca brought two worlds together. The maritime empire of Srivijaya was located here at a cultural crossroads between East and West. From its location on the southeast coast of Sumatra, Srivijaya monopolized trade that passed through the Strait of Malacca. Traders from China, India, and the Arabian Peninsula anchored at Srivijaya, where they exchanged cargoes of exotic goods for spices. Srivijaya did not hold a vast territory, but it maintained control over international trade in the Southeast Asian archipelago. During the 1500s, long after Srivijaya's decline, the Portuguese gained control of the trade that passed through the strait.

Portuguese Trade in Malacca

At this time there was a large number of merchants of many nationalities in Malacca, . . . the merchants and sea-traders realised how much difference there was in sailing to Malacca, because they could anchor safely there in all weathers, and could buy from the others when it was convenient. They began to come to Malacca all the time because they got returns.

—Tome Pires, in *Suma Oriental*, early 1500s

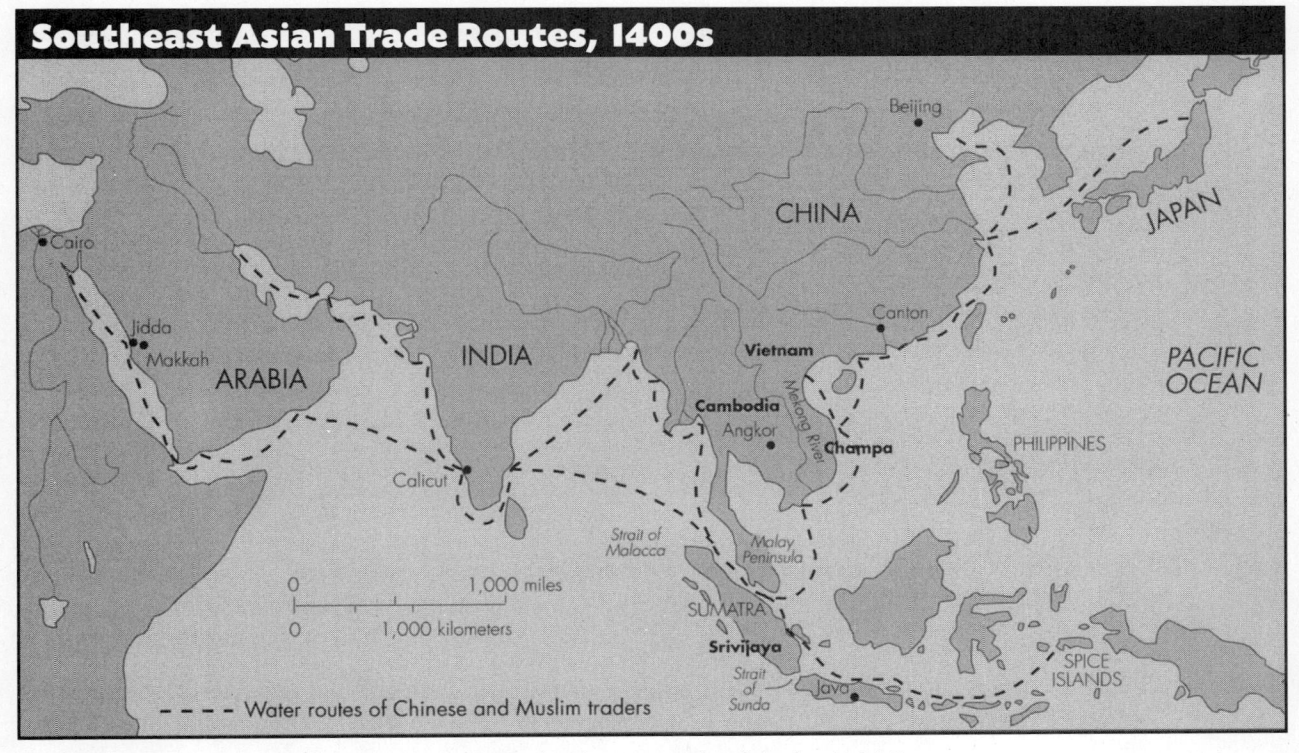

Southeast Asian Trade Routes, 1400s

Islamic and Chinese traders sailed through the Strait of Malacca to reach safe harbor in Srivijaya.

World History　　　　　Geography and History Activities　　**27**

Name _____ Date _____ Class _____

GEOGRAPHY and HISTORY Activity 14

Focus on Location

People choose to settle in certain locations for many reasons. Soil, climate, and energy sources provide the basic elements for human survival. If an area also has navigable rivers and deep harbors, those geographic features allow people to transport goods and passengers to other markets or population centers.

Distant resources and markets can also influence the location of settlements. Srivijaya's position on the Strait of Malacca enabled it to control trade coming from the East and the West. When the Portuguese, and later the Dutch, realized the profits that could be made by monopolizing the spice trade of the Indonesian archipelago, they quickly established forts and warehouses on the Malay Peninsula. Forts protected the Portuguese trading ships and secured the area against other European powers.

1. What factors affect the location of a settlement?

   _____

2. Why might the advantages of a location not be apparent to a visitor?

   _____
   _____

3. What natural resource was sought by Islamic, Indian, and Chinese traders?

   _____

4. What does Tome Pires's account reveal about the relationship between location and the economy of Indonesian islands?

   _____
   _____

Critical Thinking

5. **Drawing Conclusions** After the Portuguese established a trading center in Malacca, they went on to set up trading posts in China and Japan. Why were they interested in those locations?

   _____
   _____

6. **Making Inferences** Srivijaya attracted many diverse cultures to its ports. Which cultural elements do you think might have been adopted by the native populations of Sumatra?

   _____
   _____

Activity

7. Look for articles in newspapers, news magazines, or geographic magazines that describe the economic activities of Indonesia today. Explain in a brief report how Indonesia's location is related to its economy.

Name .... Date .... Geography .... Class ....

GEOGRAPHY and HISTORY Activity 15

Human-Environment Interaction: *What's for Dinner?*

As early peoples moved across North America, different groups settled in different regions. People who settled in particular regions developed distinctive cultures. The cultures of northern North Americans reflected their local geography and natural resources.

The diets of early people of the Americas were determined by two factors: locally available food sources and the crops they were able to grow. Along the Pacific coast of North America, people depended mainly on the sea as a source of food. They hunted whales and seals and fished for salmon and bass. They also ate berries and acorns found in the forest, but they did not plant crops. The people who lived in the Southwest hunted small animals, such as birds and rabbits. They also grew kidney beans, squash, and—most important—maize.

Maize was first grown about 7,000 years ago near what is now Mexico City. Scientists believe that this grain was intentionally developed by early farmers through a process of careful breeding. From Mesoamerica, maize spread north. By the time the first Europeans arrived in the Americas, this staple crop was grown as far north as southern Canada and as far east as the land along the Mississippi River. Maize was such an important crop that people found ways to improve its cultivation. In the Southwest, people developed irrigation methods to bring water into the dry areas and a system of terraces to control erosion in steeply sloped areas.

> *Columbus and the innumerable discoveries that followed his venture across the Atlantic changed many things for the inhabitants of the Old World, but for most people what mattered most was not the new information about the lands, peoples, plants, and animals . . . nor was it the gold and silver treasure. . . . Instead it was a change that historians have often overlooked: the spread of American food crops to Europe, Asia, and Africa.*
> —William H. McNeill, "American Food Crops in the Old World"

Maize is not one kind of plant but a group of many varieties. Different varieties produce kernels that are white, yellow, red, brown, and even blue.

World History — Geography and History Activities — **29**

Name _____ Date _____ Class _____

GEOGRAPHY and HISTORY Activity 15

Focus on Human-Environment Interaction

The plants in an environment affect the culture of the people who settle there. But the people also affect the environment. Farming brings many changes to an environment. In choosing one plant as a crop, people choose not to grow others. Removing some kinds of plants to grow others can affect the mineral content of the soil. It also affects local animal populations by taking away the preferred food of certain animals. In addition, farming changes the landforms in an environment. Irrigation channels interrupt once-unbroken fields. Terraces change the slope of a hillside.

1. How does the geography of a region affect what people eat?

2. List some ways that people's efforts to get food might affect the geography of where they live.

3. Why do you think the Arctic peoples did not grow any crops?

4. Why did farming peoples such as the Pueblo live in villages while nonfarmers such as the Crow, who lived mainly on bison, did not?

Critical Thinking

5. **Making Inferences** What other aspects of culture might be affected by a region's geography?

6. **Making Inferences** What factors besides geography might affect the culture of a people?

Activity

7. Research the Native Americans who lived in your area before 1500. What was their diet like? What were some other ways that they used the geography and natural resources of the area? How did they change the geography?

Name .... Date .... Class ....

GEOGRAPHY and HISTORY Activity 16

Movement: *Venice, Queen of the Adriatic*

"*Desponsamus te, mare*" (We wed thee, O sea), exclaimed the doge of Venice, standing at the bow of the state gallery and hurling a consecrated gold ring into the Adriatic Sea. In Renaissance Venice, this symbolic marriage of the city to the sea was performed each year in a splendid water festival that included choirs, trumpets, banners, and a flotilla of gondolas. How did Venice become Queen of the Adriatic—the commercial center of the world at that time?

The city of Venice reached its commercial and political power and glory as a trading center during the 1300s and 1400s. The French ambassador Philippe de Comines in 1495 called Venice's Grand Canal the "handsomest avenue . . . in the whole world." Venetian merchants crowded the canals with their gondolas filled with all manner of goods. "There were so many boats it seemed as if all the gardens of the world must be there," remarked a merchant from Milan when he saw the maze of market boats loaded with produce from the mainland. Far more valuable goods than vegetables, however, were traded on the Venetian canals.

Venice was the hub of commercial activity for the whole Mediterranean. Fleets of merchant ships set out from the northern Adriatic, in the heart of Europe, to move large quantities of diverse products throughout the Mediterranean and Black Seas. Sailors loaded tons of precious East Indian spices onto their ships in Alexandria and Beirut to be sold in places as far away as England. Some fleets loaded furs, silks, and dyes from Black Sea ports; others carried wool and leather from Spain; and still others transported enslaved people, gold, and ivory from Africa. Christian pilgrims boarded Venetian ships to sail to the Holy Land. Venetian trade routes began and ended in Venice—the center of the wealthiest trading network in Europe. A medieval monk complained that St. Mark's Square "seems perpetually filled with Turks, Libyans, and Parthians," evidence of Venice's cosmopolitan character even in its early days. As Venetians moved goods and people across the Mediterranean Sea, cultural and political ideologies traveled with them and spread throughout the region.

> *Sun-grit city, thou hast been*
> *Ocean's child, and then his queen;*
> *Now is come a darker day,*
> *And thou soon must be his prey.*
> —Percy Bysshe Shelley, "Lines written amongst the Euganean Hills," 1818

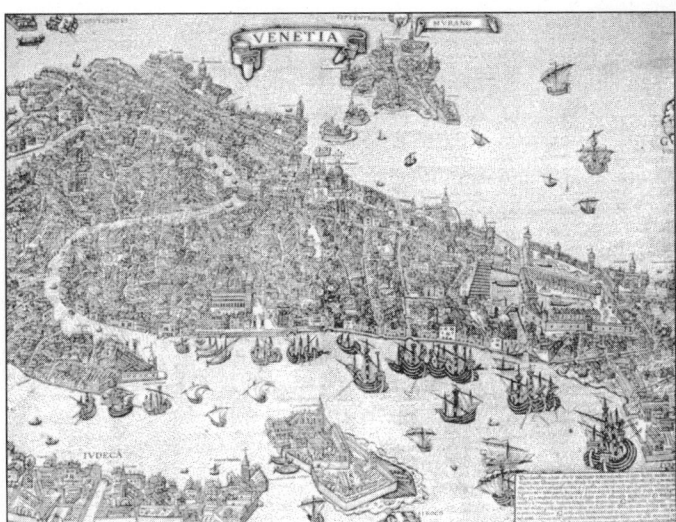

Venice is located on 120 islands in the Adriatic Sea, separated from Italy's mainland by a lagoon. A system of canals branch off the Grand Canal, clearly visible in this 1500 engraving by Jacopo Dei Barberi. A large complex of shipyards once dominated the eastern tip of the city. There, shipwrights constructed the merchant ships that sailed from Venice to all major ports in the Mediterranean.

World History   Geography and History Activities   **31**

Name .... Date .... Class ....

GEOGRAPHY and HISTORY
Activity 16

Focus on Movement

Human movement, initiated by human needs and wants, can create patterns and centers of activity. Situated on the Mediterranean Sea and also midway between the markets of Asia and western Europe, Venice used its advantageous location to establish Mediterranean trade routes linking these markets. Trade movement brought goods as well as money to Venice, making the city a great commercial center where banking, shipbuilding, and maritime-supply industries thrived. Later, the Portuguese established an Asian trade route around Africa, bypassing the Venetian trade network. Then the center of commercial activity moved from Venice to several cities located along the Atlantic coast.

1. How does human movement create patterns and centers of activity?

   _____
   _____

2. How did Venice's role in the Mediterranean trade network affect commercial life in the city?

   _____
   _____

3. Study the engraving on the previous page and explain the advantage of having the Grand Canal run through the city.

   _____

4. How did Venice's geographic location lead to its becoming an important trading center?

   _____

Critical Thinking

5. **Making Comparisons** Venetian ships covered thousands of miles in the Mediterranean and Black Seas as they followed trade routes. Compare the movement of Venetian ships in the 1300s to the movement of Islamic caravans carrying salt and gold to and from Ghana at about the same time.

   _____
   _____

6. **Determining Relevance** The expectation of financial profits motivated the Venetians to send fleets throughout the Mediterranean and Black Seas. List other factors that motivate people to move themselves, goods, or ideas from one place to another.

   _____
   _____

Activity

7. Use an atlas to locate the places where Venetian fleets traveled. Start with a list of the places mentioned on the previous page. Then research to find the largest trading centers in the world today and locate them on maps.

Name .... Date .... Class ....

GEOGRAPHY and HISTORY Activity 17

Location: *Columbus's Landfall*

When a cannon's thunder rumbled over the moonlit waters, Christopher Columbus knew his prayers had been answered. His lead ship had sighted land. Columbus had navigated three small caravels across the Atlantic Ocean in 33 days. What was Columbus hoping he had found?

Columbus's landing on a Caribbean island he called San Salvador (Holy Savior) has been called one of the most significant events in modern history. But where did he actually land? Historians disagree on the site of his landfall.

Cartographers have identified 723 islands in the Bahamas, where Columbus's western course took him. In his log, Columbus described what island inhabitants told him—using gestures and names in their language—about the surrounding area. He also recorded his own observations of the islands. Using Columbus's log, historians have compared descriptions of the islands with bearings of courses he sailed to determine which island was Columbus's San Salvador.

Log of Christopher Columbus

Friday, 12 October 1492
Tomorrow afternoon I intend to go to the SW. The natives have indicated to me that not only is there land to the south and SW, but also to the NW. I shall go to the SW and look for gold and precious stones. . . .
This island is fairly large and very flat. It is green, with many trees and several bodies of water. There is a very large lagoon in the middle of the island and there are no mountains. It is a pleasure to gaze upon this place because it is all so green, and the weather is delightful.

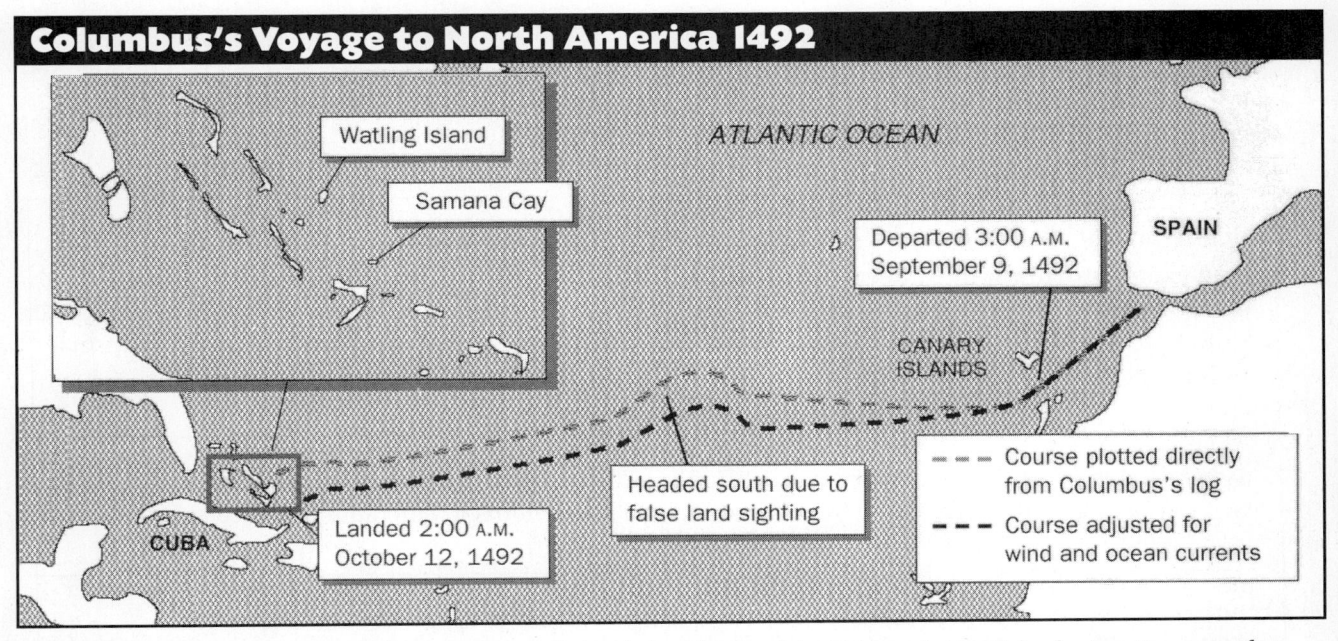

Columbus's Voyage to North America 1492

- Watling Island
- Samana Cay
- ATLANTIC OCEAN
- Departed 3:00 A.M. September 9, 1492
- SPAIN
- CANARY ISLANDS
- Headed south due to false land sighting
- CUBA
- Landed 2:00 A.M. October 12, 1492
- --- Course plotted directly from Columbus's log
- --- Course adjusted for wind and ocean currents

Using the Columbus log for bearings and distances traveled each day, historian John McElroy charted Columbus's entire voyage from the Canary Islands to the Bahamas. His calculations placed landfall at Watling Island. When sailor-scientist Luis Marden calculated the course, he realized that McElroy had not included the effects of wind and ocean currents. These adjustments placed landfall 10 miles to the southeast—on Samana Cay.

World History

Name .... Date .... Class ....

GEOGRAPHY and HISTORY Activity 17

Focus on Location

There are different answers to the question "Where is it?" You can give the location of a place by describing its absolute location or its relative location. Absolute location identifies the exact site using a grid, such as latitude and longitude. Relative location identifies location in terms of other landmarks. The Columbus log does not give the absolute location of San Salvador. However, it indicates the location of San Salvador relative to the Canary Islands far to the east and to the nearby Bahamian islands.

Modern historians have tried to use the relative locations given in the Columbus log to pinpoint the absolute location of San Salvador. Luis Marden believes the absolute location is at 23°09'00"N latitude and 73°29'13"W longitude.

1. What is the difference between absolute location and relative location?

2. Describe the relative location of San Salvador.

3. What is the absolute location of Columbus's San Salvador, according to Luis Marden?

4. Which features in Columbus's description of San Salvador would help identify the island of his landfall?

5. The Columbus log gives additional details about his contact with islanders and the rest of his voyage around the Bahamas. What additional information would you want from the log in order to confirm the location of San Salvador?

Critical Thinking

6. **Analyzing Information** In deep waters of the Mediterranean, navigators during the time of Columbus used the compass to pilot their ships. In northern Europe, where the water is shallower, sailors dropped lines overboard to determine how deep the water was. How might this information have helped them navigate?

7. **Synthesizing Information** Every day, Columbus calculated the distance he traveled using a log, a rope, and a clock. Describe how you think he used these items to calculate distance.

Activity

8. With your classmates, brainstorm a list of European explorers who, like Columbus, changed history. How did their explorations change the lives of people in Europe and around the world?

34   Geography and History Activities   World History

Name _____ Date _____ Class _____

GEOGRAPHY and HISTORY Activity 18

Region: *In the Shogun's Grip*

Hideyoshi, the warlord who had united all Japan, stopped his horse and gestured toward the head of Edo Bay. "Make your capital there," he said to Tokugawa Ieyasu. How did the rich Edo region fit into Ieyasu's plans to rule the region himself one day?

Ieyasu crushed the power of the Hideyoshi family in 1600. Soon he ruled from Edo as shogun, supreme military commander. Edo, at first a little fishing village on the bay, grew rapidly into a city of 500,000 inhabitants centered on a circular fortress two miles in diameter. It commanded the broad Kanto Plain, the richest farm region in rocky Japan. Tokugawa shoguns continued to add territory until they directly controlled as much as a third of Japan's people and a third or more of its agricultural wealth. Even the emperor's capital, Kyoto, belonged to the shoguns.

The shogun gave other daimyos control only in their own domains. He also issued strict laws to keep the daimyos in the shogun region isolated and weak.

Laws Governing Daimyos, 1615

Great lords, the lesser lords, and officials should immediately expel from their domains any among their retainers or henchmen who have been charged with treason or murder.
Henceforth no outsider, none but the inhabitants of a particular domain, shall be permitted to reside in that domain. . . .
Immediate report should be made of . . . factional conspiracies being formed in neighboring domains.

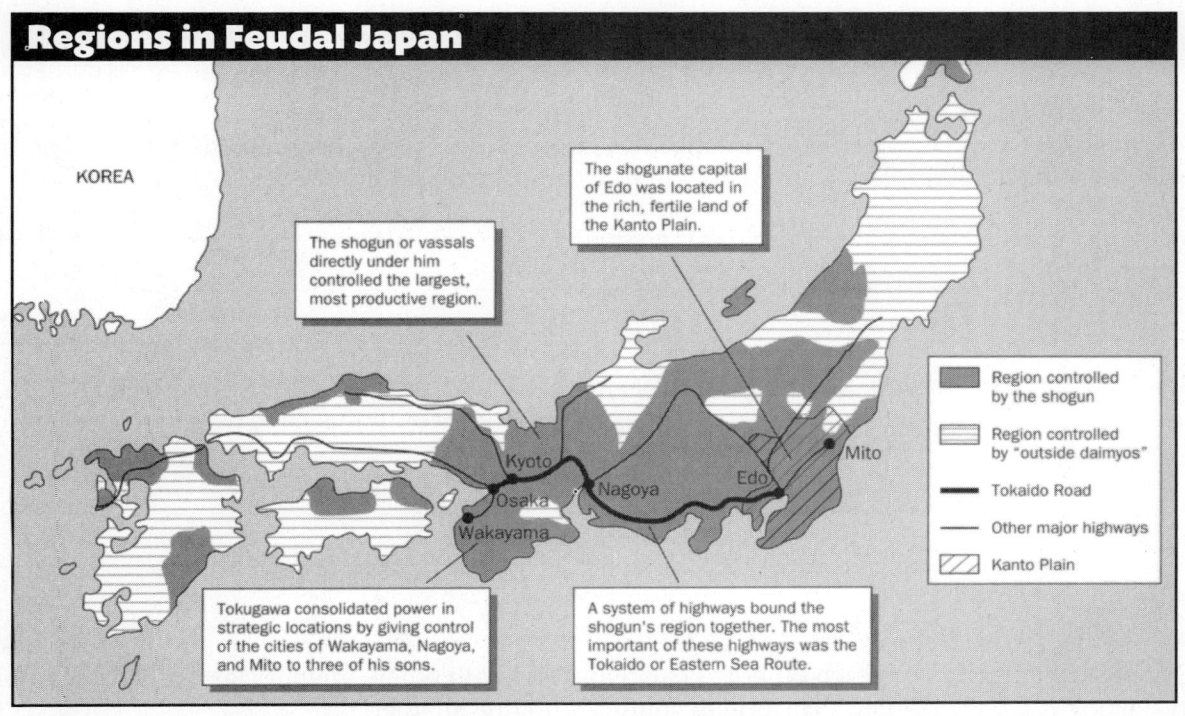

Regions in Feudal Japan

KOREA

The shogunate capital of Edo was located in the rich, fertile land of the Kanto Plain.

The shogun or vassals directly under him controlled the largest, most productive region.

Kyoto • Nagoya • Edo • Mito
Osaka
Wakayama

- Region controlled by the shogun
- Region controlled by "outside daimyos"
- Tokaido Road
- Other major highways
- Kanto Plain

Tokugawa consolidated power in strategic locations by giving control of the cities of Wakayama, Nagoya, and Mito to three of his sons.

A system of highways bound the shogun's region together. The most important of these highways was the Tokaido or Eastern Sea Route.

The vast Edo region was defined by the Tokaido Road running through the shogun's domains. The road served as a visual manifestation of the extent of the shogun's power.

World History — Geography and History Activities **35**

Name .... Date .... Class ....

GEOGRAPHY and HISTORY Activity 18

Focus on Region

Because any feature, either natural or human-made, can define a region, it is no surprise that regions can take almost any shape or size. Political features defined regions of feudal Japan. Hundreds of daimyos held domains of varying sizes. Some of these political units could also belong to a far larger and more powerful region controlled by the shogun. The Tokugawa shogunate controlled a major portion of Japan. The policy of the shogunate was to centralize shogun power and keep daimyo power fragmented. The smaller domains of the daimyos were essentially individual regions, cut off from one another so that they could never combine against the shogun. So successful was this scheme that the Tokugawa shogunate lasted until 1867.

1. Why do regions vary in size?

2. What determined the power of Japanese feudal regions?

3. How did the shogun ensure that traitors would have no base from which to operate?

4. Explain how both the size and the location of the region held by the shogun helped him control the daimyos.

Critical Thinking

5. **Making Inferences** A commentary on the laws governing daimyos suggested that the customs of each domain should be secret. What do you think was the reason for this?

6. **Synthesizing Information** Japanese daimyos, required to spend considerable time at Edo, traveled often between their domains and the capital. How would this have helped the Japanese economy?

Activity

7. As you can see from the example of feudal Japan, regions are often defined by power and politics. Regions can interact with each other to change history. With others in your class, discuss examples of regions you have studied that were in conflict with one another.

Geography and History Activity 19

Human-Environment Interaction: *Dutch Masters*

A patchwork of red and yellow tulips, green pastureland, and acres of glass greenhouses surround small suburban towns and several large cities in the Netherlands today. Driven by the need to keep the North Sea from flooding their country, the Dutch have become masters at reclaiming land. Hundreds of acres of reclaimed land exist because the Dutch have managed to change the geography of their country by controlling their environment. How have the changing needs of the Dutch people affected the landscape of their country?

Beginning about 1200, Dutch farmers attempted to halt destruction of coastal dune areas by building dikes—large sea barriers made from rock and clay that kept the North Sea from cutting through the dunes and inundating their farmland. By the 1500s, the Dutch required even more farmland to feed a growing population. So they reclaimed the marshy lowlands by building dikes around a parcel of land and then used windmills to pump the water into canals. Farmers called the areas of reclaimed land *polders*. A polder made ideal pastureland and allowed the Dutch to raise more and more livestock.

The Dutch people use determination and ingenuity to change their land to suit their needs. Land use today in the Netherlands is quite different from what it was in the 1300s. Conservationists and industrialists clash over issues of land use. While some people want land for recreational use, others would prefer to see land made available for housing or industrial development.

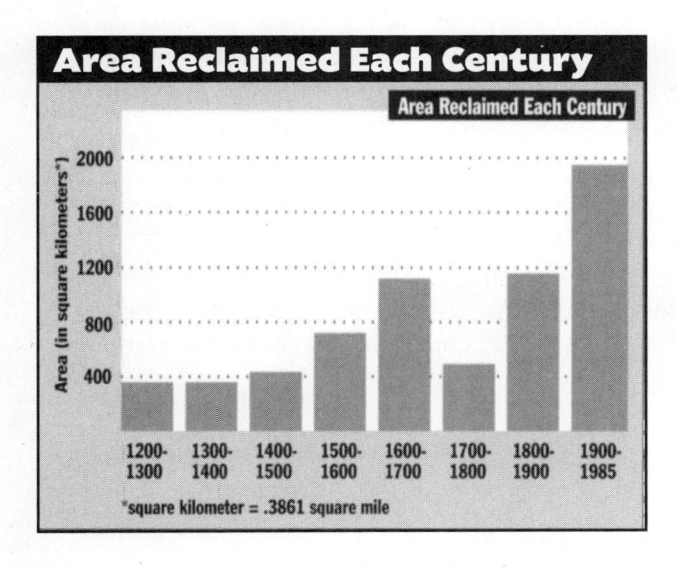

Area Reclaimed Each Century

*square kilometer = .3861 square mile

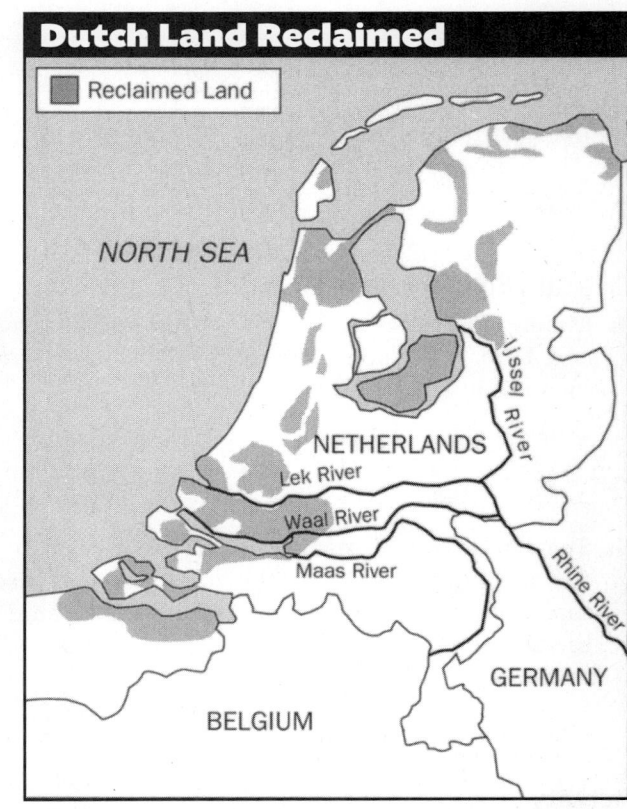

Dutch Land Reclaimed

World History Geography and History Activities **37**

Name _____ Date _____ Class _____

GEOGRAPHY and HISTORY Activity 19

Focus on Human-Environment Interaction

Humans have always interacted with their environment to meet their immediate needs for food, shelter, and clothing. As their needs change over time, people find new ways to interact with their environment. For example, people employed primarily in agriculture need arable land, but urbanites need open recreational land where they can exercise, relax, and play. Today, the government of the Netherlands is concerned about the effects of pollution on the environment and have embarked on plans to modify land use once again. A 1989 report issued by the Information and Documentation Centre for the Geography of the Netherlands suggested multiple uses for agricultural land, including recreation areas and conservation land.

1. How is the environment affected by changing human needs?

   _____
   _____

2. What geographic features of the Netherlands caused the Dutch to begin reclaiming land?

   _____
   _____

3. Look at the graph on page 37. Describe the land reclamation activity between 1200 and 1500.

   _____
   _____

Critical Thinking

4. **Making Inferences** The golden years of Dutch commerce and influence occurred between 1600 and 1700. Make some inferences about how the events of that century contributed to the huge increase in land reclamation.

   _____
   _____

5. **Synthesizing Information** Until this century, the Dutch have used polder land primarily for agricultural purposes. Today the government is discussing multiple uses for lands, such as agriculture, recreation, and conservation. What would be the environmental advantages of diversifying the use of agricultural land in the Netherlands?

   _____
   _____

Activity

6. Write a brief report focusing on the effects of human-environment interactions in your community. Give examples of how your community has changed its use of land in the past and how it may in the future as a result of changing human needs.

Name .... Date .... Class ....

GEOGRAPHY and HISTORY Activity 20

Location: *Where Is the World?*

In 1543, Polish astronomer Nicolaus Copernicus lay dying when his friends placed the first bound copy of his book, *On the Revolutions of Celestial Spheres*, in his frail hands. Copernicus stared at the book and then at his friends and said nothing. No one knew if Copernicus realized what he held. Who could have known that the ideas in the book would forever change people's thinking about the universe?

During the time of Copernicus, European ideas about the universe had come from the teachings of ancient Greeks—teachings that had been formulated nearly 1,400 years earlier. The Greek astronomer Ptolemy had taught that the earth stood still at the center of the universe and that all other spheres revolved around it. The Catholic Church reinforced this view. According to the Church, the earth, where humans lived, was the greatest planet in God's universe; all other planets revolved around it.

Copernicus's studies of the movement of planets led him to challenge this theory. He came to believe that the sun, not the earth, was at the center of the universe. All the planets, including the earth, revolved around the sun. Yet Copernicus was afraid to publish his ideas lest he be branded a heretic and punished by the Church. He continued his studies in isolation.

With the publication of his ideas at his death, Copernicus launched later scientists into new investigations about the universe. No longer tied to the Church's view and to outdated teachings, astronomers such as Galileo and Kepler would prove that Copernicus was indeed right—the earth and the other planets revolved around the sun. These new ideas and a growing interest in the natural world marked the beginning of the Scientific Revolution that transformed people's thinking in the 1600s.

Copernicus's Universe

In the middle of everything is the sun. For in this most beautiful temple, who would place this lamp in another or better position than that from which it can light up the whole thing at the same time? . . . Thus indeed, as though seated on a royal throne, the sun rules the family of planets revolving around it.

—Nicolaus Copernicus, in *On the Revolutions of Celestial Spheres*, 1543

This diagram illustrates Copernicus's radical new view of the universe.

World History — Geography and History Activities — 39

Name _____ Date _____ Class _____

GEOGRAPHY and HISTORY Activity 20

Focus on Location

As you have learned, location can be described by compass directions or in terms of relation to other landmarks. You can, for example, tell someone your house is two blocks to the east of where you are now standing. Or, depending on the person's familiarity with the area, you may say that your home is just around the corner from Town Hall. Often the description of a location reflects the point of view of a person or a group. In Copernicus's day, the description of the location of the earth and the universe itself reflected the views held by the Roman Catholic Church and by Greek teachings that were thousands of years old.

Today we find that the descriptions of many locations continue to reflect the viewpoints of particular groups and individuals. Why do people in the United States still refer to Asia as the "Far East"? In fact, it is easier for Americans to reach those countries by going west.

1. Why might people give different descriptions of the location of a place?
   _____

2. Why did the Catholic Church believe that the earth stood in the middle of the universe?
   _____

3. What led Copernicus to challenge the view that the earth was at the center of the universe?
   _____

4. Why was Copernicus reluctant to make his views public?
   _____

5. Why is it a good idea to determine a person's familiarity with an area before giving him or her a description of a location?
   _____
   _____

Critical Thinking

6. **Drawing Conclusions** In what sense can Copernicus be called a revolutionary?
   _____

7. **Recognizing Ideologies** How do institutions today mold the way people think about places in the world? Use examples from your own experience with institutions such as the government, schools, and church organizations to explain your answer.
   _____

Activity

8. As a class, conduct a survey. Ask five people to describe the location of these places: Mexico, Russia, Ethiopia, Switzerland, and China. Compare your findings. What do the descriptions of the locations tell you about the perspectives of the direction-givers?

40   Geography and History Activities   World History

Name _____ Date _____ Class _____

GEOGRAPHY and HISTORY Activity 21

Region: *Looking at the Land*

European explorers set sail with dreams of glory and discovery in the late 1400s. The vast wilderness of the Americas held the promise of great riches. What form these riches took—gold, furs, or land for settlement—depended on the perception of the adventurer. How did the adventurers' views reflect the goals of the countries they sailed for?

Spanish explorers searched for landscapes in the Americas similar to those of their European homeland. Spaniards had learned to mine the mineral ores from Spain's low mountainous terrain. Knowing the importance of metallurgy to the Spanish economy, the earliest Spanish explorers were drawn to the mountainous areas of Mexico and what is today the southwest United States, where mining operations could be established quickly. They were more eager to make quick profits from mining than to develop self-sufficient colonies based on an agricultural economy.

The French, too, were eager for the profits they could make from North America's natural resources, but they were forced to search in northern North America, because the Spanish had already claimed much of Central America and South America. French explorers Jacques Cartier and Samuel de Champlain had explored the St. Lawrence River system and the northern Appalachian area, claiming those places for France. Finding a region teeming with beaver, muskrat, and deer, the French turned to trading metal knives, tools, and guns for furs from animals hunted by Native Americans. The French built a fur-trading monopoly that brought them great wealth without the problems of clearing, farming, and settling the rocky lands of northern New England and Canada.

The English, however, found a land and climate in Virginia that was better suited than their homeland for growing food and producing simple products from the abundance of raw materials available in North America. English colonies of the 1600s grew into farm communities that traded farm products for manufactured English goods.

The English Perception

"There are valleys and plains streaming with the sweet springs.... The land is full of minerals and plenty of woods, of which we have a lack in England. There are growing goodly oaks and elms, beech and birch ... and fir trees in great abundance. The soil is strong and lusty of its own nature."
—Anonymous English writer, early 1600s

The French Perception

"There is a great number of stags, deer, bears, rabbits, foxes, otters, beavers, weasels, badgers and ... many other sorts of wild beasts."
—Jacques Cartier, 1530s

The Spanish Perception

"The discovery of the South Sea would lead to the discovery of many islands rich in gold, pearls, precious stones ... and other unknown and wonderful things."
—Hernán Cortés, 1533

European claims to land in North America led to a variety of settlement patterns—from rough wilderness camps to sprawling coastal plantations.

1713
- English claims
- French claims
- Spanish claims

World History

Name _____ Date _____ Class _____

GEOGRAPHY and HISTORY Activity 21

Focus on Region

The different ways in which the Spanish, French, and English explored and colonized the Americas reflect their differing perceptions of the regions. Spanish explorers were enticed to search for legendary cities such as El Dorado, where the streets were said to be paved with gold, and the Seven Cities of Cíbola, which allegedly held enormous treasures. Their dreams of finding these places gave explorers the determination to face hardships and disappointments. French explorers, however, looked at North America as a place where fortunes could be made from the fur trade. Settlements were temporary hunting communities, quite different from English farming colonies, where families had migrated to start a new life in a new land.

1. What makes people perceive regions differently?

2. What North American resources were important to the Spanish, the French, and the English?

3. What circumstances in Europe made the English so delighted to find good farmland in North America?

4. How would the popular fashion of beaver hats in Europe in the 1500s have affected the French who came to North America?

Critical Thinking

5. **Making Inferences** The Spanish claimed more of the Americas than the French and English combined. What historical event gave the Spanish an advantage in their claims?

6. **Synthesizing Information** The English adventurer and sailor Sir Francis Drake captured numerous Spanish ships in the early 1500s. Why were the English interested in taking the cargoes of Spanish ships?

Activity

7. With a partner, select a region of the world and then write separate one-page descriptions of what you think are the important aspects of that region. When you finish writing, compare your perceptions. How are they similar and how are they different?

GEOGRAPHY and HISTORY Activity 22

Movement: *A Doomed March to Russia*

Napoleon gathered troops from all quarters of his European empire in his quest to conquer the Russian Empire. By June 1812 his "Grand Army," numbering 600,000 men, confidently began to march east across the vast, level Russian plain. Yet six months later, these same troops were making a desperate escape from Russia—having lost more than 400,000 men. What caused this panicked retreat and massive loss of life?

Napoleon had underestimated the Russian troops and his most bitter rival, the fierce Russian winter. To resist Napoleon, the Russians used a new strategy. Instead of meeting the French in open battle, the Russian army retreated slowly, drawing the French army deeper and deeper into Russia.

In September, Napoleon's forces finally reached Moscow, which the Russians had evacuated. The day after the French entered Moscow, a huge fire, probably started by Russian patriots, destroyed the city. With the Russian winter looming, Napoleon faced a difficult decision. He could either chase the Russian army farther to the east or turn back to the west.

Napoleon waited too long to make his decision to retreat. Bitter cold and driving snow plagued the Grand Army as it crossed the vast Russian plain once again. Temperatures plunged and Russians began attacking French forces without mercy.

The Grand Army's Retreat

The strongest threw into the river those who were weaker, and . . . trampled underfoot all the sick whom they found in their way. . . . Others, hoping to save themselves by swimming, were frozen in the middle of the river, or perished by placing themselves on pieces of ice, which sunk to the bottom. Thousands and thousands . . . were lost.
—French officer's account

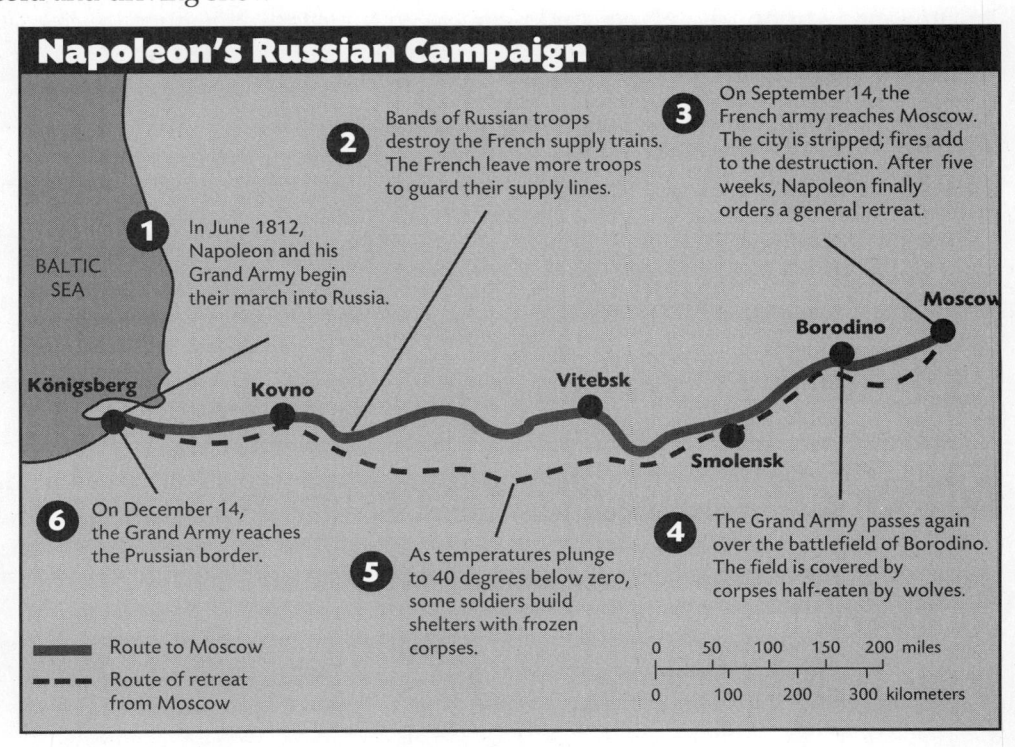

With the help of the severe winter of their homeland, Russian forces wiped out most of the Grand Army by the time it returned to Germany in December 1812.

Napoleon's Russian Campaign

1. In June 1812, Napoleon and his Grand Army begin their march into Russia.
2. Bands of Russian troops destroy the French supply trains. The French leave more troops to guard their supply lines.
3. On September 14, the French army reaches Moscow. The city is stripped; fires add to the destruction. After five weeks, Napoleon finally orders a general retreat.
4. The Grand Army passes again over the battlefield of Borodino. The field is covered by corpses half-eaten by wolves.
5. As temperatures plunge to 40 degrees below zero, some soldiers build shelters with frozen corpses.
6. On December 14, the Grand Army reaches the Prussian border.

Locations: Baltic Sea, Königsberg, Kovno, Vitebsk, Smolensk, Borodino, Moscow

— Route to Moscow
--- Route of retreat from Moscow

Scale: 0–200 miles / 0–300 kilometers

Name _____ Date _____ Class _____

GEOGRAPHY and HISTORY Activity 22

Focus on Movement

Throughout history, people have moved from one location to another to fulfill specific needs. Sometimes the movement is economically motivated, such as the search for better jobs. Napoleon's march on Russia had another motive—to conquer the Russian Empire.

Geographic barriers, such as the Russian winter that stood in the way of Napoleon's plans, have prevented people from moving from one location to another. Mountains, rivers, and deserts are other physical factors that have hindered movement.

Today, technological advances in communication and transportation allow people to overcome many of these physical barriers. Yet other barriers exist. Repressive governments often deny their citizens the freedom to move to other countries. In addition, immigration laws and regulations keep people around the world from freely moving to other nations.

1. What are different kinds of barriers to movement?

   _____

   _____

2. According to the map on page 43, approximately how many miles did the Grand Army march in order to reach Moscow? How long did it take to cover this distance?

   _____

   _____

3. How many troops did Napoleon lose between June and December 1812?

   _____

4. How has the nature of barriers to movement changed?

   _____

   _____

Critical Thinking

5. **Drawing Conclusions** The Russian army destroyed everything that might be of use to the French—even the city of Moscow. What do you think were the consequences of this policy for the Russian people? What alternative strategies might Russian leaders have considered?

   _____

6. **Analyzing Information** How might geographical barriers to movement hinder a nation's development? How might they help it?

   _____

Activity

7. Research the settlement of the area in which you live. What factors encouraged settlement? What factors prohibited settlement? What affects the movement of people in and out of your area today?

Name .... Date .... Class ....

GEOGRAPHY and HISTORY Activity 23

Human-Environment Interaction: *A Big Ditch or a Grand Canal?*

President Thomas Jefferson thought the idea was crazy, and in 1809 he refused to fund the project with federal money. Attempting to carve the Erie Canal through the New York wilderness was "little short of madness," Jefferson fumed. But New York governor De Witt Clinton refused to let the plan die. He remained determined to construct the canal—making water travel from the Great Lakes to the Atlantic Ocean a reality. How would Governor Clinton carry out his plan?

Clinton called on his fellow New Yorkers to fund a $7 million canal that would link Buffalo to New York City via Albany and the Hudson River. Engineers who had studied Great Britain's canals developed the plans, and construction began in 1817. More than 3,000 workers cleared trees, leveled ground, and dug the ditch for the canal, which would cover 350 miles and raise and lower boats nearly 600 feet during their journey.

When construction ended in 1825, the canal was an immediate success. The cost of shipping grain from Lake Erie to the Atlantic dropped from $100 to $20 a ton, and the time in transit was cut from 20 to 8 days. The Erie Canal carried such a volume that it repaid its initial cost within 12 years. It also helped New York City develop into the nation's financial center. No longer known as Clinton's "Big Ditch," the new waterway was soon billed as America's "Grand Canal."

Digging the Big Ditch

"We are digging the Ditch through the mire;
Through the mud and the slime and the mire,
 by heck!
And the mud is our principal hire;
Up our pants, in our shirts, down our neck,
 by heck!
We are digging the Ditch through the gravel,
So the people and freight can travel."
—Erie Canal work song

Erie Canal workers excavate a deep cut. Dug in rough, sparsely settled wilderness, the canal progressed about a mile a week. Since the elevation of Lake Erie was 565 feet (172 meters) higher than the Hudson River at Albany, the Erie Canal had 83 locks with lifts that raised and lowered the boats as they traveled the waterway. The locks became the marvels of their day.

World History · Geography and History Activities · **45**

Name .... Date .... Class ....

GEOGRAPHY and HISTORY Activity 23

Focus on Human-Environment Interaction

Through imagination, technology, and hard work, people have been able to alter their environments to suit their needs. Different cultures tend to approach the environment in different ways. Whereas Native Americans felt at one with the environment, European settlers regarded it as something to use or tame. In the United States, Americans have dramatically transformed their environment, tunneling railroad passages through the Sierra Nevada and diverting water from the Colorado River to desert regions. Projects such as the Erie Canal linked waterways, easing transportation and spurring industrial development. The model of the British canal system enabled Americans to envision and build a canal in an area where Native Americans had used the existing waterways for hundreds of years.

1. What approach did European settlers in America often take toward their physical environment?

2. What was the goal of the Erie Canal project?

3. Name some of the geographic obstacles developers had to consider before beginning the canal.

4. Why do you think Clinton was willing to risk building the canal despite Jefferson's doubts?

5. What effect do you think the Erie Canal had on the development of industry in New York State? On other canal projects in the United States?

Critical Thinking

6. **Formulating Questions** Why would the canal developers have studied the British canal system before they designed the Erie Canal? Write four questions the developers might have asked during their studies.

7. **Drawing Conclusions** Why do you think some cultures transformed their physical environment more than others?

Activity

8. Read the local newspaper and look for an ongoing project in which people are altering their environment. Identify the project's goal. Does everyone in the area agree with the project and its goals? What are some objections? Do you think the project will be successful? Why or why not?

GEOGRAPHY and HISTORY Activity 24

Place: *Population Time Bomb*

In the 1700s Great Britain's population began to increase rapidly for a number of reasons, including the availability of better food and improved hygiene and sanitation practices. This population boom concerned many British people, among them Thomas Malthus, a clergyman and economist. The population figures puzzled Malthus. Was the population increase a sign of progress or impending disaster?

In 1798 Malthus published his answer. In a book entitled *An Essay on the Principle of Population*, he argued that population would increase so rapidly that it would outstrip society's ability to provide the necessities of life. Population, he wrote, grows in geometrical ratio (1, 2, 4, 8, 16) while food supply increases in arithmetical ratio (1, 2, 3, 4, 5). Unless people limited the size of their families, Malthus believed, poverty and food shortages would be unavoidable.

People today continue to be concerned about the growing population and the shortages of food supplies in many parts of the world. The problem of hunger has not been eradicated—neither in the cities of industrialized countries nor in developing countries where widespread famines occur.

Race Against Hunger

I say that the power of population is indefinitely greater than the power in the earth to produce subsistence for man. . . .
—Thomas Malthus, 1798

The increase in population all over the rich world may get a little less. In the poor world . . . the food-population collision will duly occur. The attempts to prevent it or meliorate it will be too feeble. Famine will take charge in many countries. . . . There will be suffering and desperation on a scale as yet unknown.
—C. P. Snow, *The State of Siege*, 1969

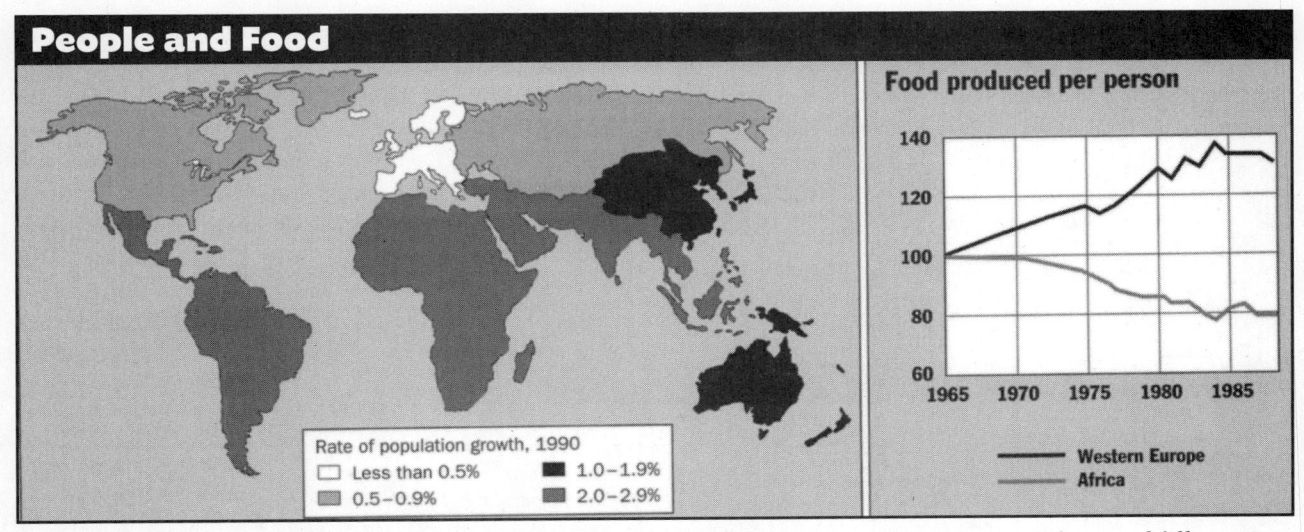

People and Food

Rate of population growth, 1990
- Less than 0.5%
- 0.5–0.9%
- 1.0–1.9%
- 2.0–2.9%

Food produced per person (Western Europe, Africa), 1965–1985

By the year 2025, the United Nations expects a world population of 8.5 billion. The map above shows growth rates of different regions. The graph shows how population growth rates affect the ability of continents to feed their populations. In 1988 per capita food production in Africa had fallen to 80 percent of 1965 levels.

Name .... Date .... Class ....

GEOGRAPHY and HISTORY Activity 24

Focus on Place

Just as every individual has a unique personality, so does every place. Geographers describe places in terms of physical characteristics such as landforms, bodies of water, climate, and soil. They also describe places in terms of their human characteristics, such as population and settlement patterns, because people's actions are critical in shaping the character of a place.

When geographers describe a place in terms of its population, they include information about its total population, population growth rate, population distribution, and population density (the number of people living in a given area, usually per square mile). Other ways to describe a population include written accounts about the people, or photographs depicting them visually. Descriptions and images of starving refugees reveal the relationship between population and food supply far more drastically than numbers alone.

1. What are two categories of characteristics geographers use to describe a place?

2. What figures would you need in order to describe the population of a place? Where might you find these figures for your own area?

3. Look at the map on page 47. In which areas of the world is the population growing fastest? From the graphs, what conclusions can you make about the availability of food in these areas?

4. How did Thomas Malthus view the relationship between population growth and environment?

Critical Thinking

5. **Evaluating Evidence** Some people believe that problems of hunger stem not so much from overpopulation in developing countries as from overconsumption in richer countries such as the United States. Evaluate this statement.

6. **Drawing Conclusions** According to some economists, education, not population control, is key to solving hunger and overpopulation problems in developing countries. How do you think education can combat these problems?

Activity

7. Research a developing nation in Latin America, Africa, or Asia. Describe the country in terms of its population. Is there a hunger problem in the nation? If so, how are the nation's leaders dealing with it? Present your findings to the class in a brief oral report.

GEOGRAPHY and HISTORY Activity 25

Region: *From Convict Colony to Commonwealth*

Matthew Everingham stood nervously in a British courtroom awaiting his sentence for stealing two lawbooks in July 1784. Looking down at the 14-year-old boy, the judge ordered, "Transported for seven years!" Matthew was to be among the first 775 criminals sent to a new prison colony in Australia. How would these people fare in this mostly unknown, uncharted land?

British government officials didn't seem to care. To relieve the overcrowded British prisons, the government was creating a prison colony in Australia—halfway around the world—where they hoped to rid themselves forever of people they considered troublesome lawbreakers.

The early convict-colonists faced difficult times, first enduring the grueling eight-month sea journey and later adjusting to the sweltering heat of the Australian summer and the thin, sandy Australian soil. Yet they also discovered that not far from their colony of New South Wales on Australia's eastern coast, there were rolling pastures excellent for raising sheep.

In search of more land to expand their successful sheep ranching, both the free settlers and the convicts working toward their freedom established new colonies called Victoria, Western Australia, South Australia, and Queensland. By the mid-1800s, poor British people were actually committing crimes in order to be sent to Australia! But, lured by the sale of cheap land, free settlers finally outnumbered the convict population by 1830.

The discovery of gold in New South Wales and Victoria in 1851 helped to triple Australia's population. Within a decade the total population of Australia jumped from 400,000 to more than a million people. Gold and the influx of immigrants led to industrialization, as railroad and telegraph lines were built and cities grew. Australians also began to protest the continued use of their territory as a penal colony, and Great Britain landed the last convicts there in 1867.

By the end of the 1800s, Australia was becoming one of the world's leading industrialized areas. The former convict colony entered the 1900s as a British commonwealth noted for its economic and social strength.

Australia in the Past

Give them a few acres of ground as soon as they arrive . . . with what assistance they may want to till them. Let it be here remarked that they cannot fly from the country, that they have no temptation to theft, and that they must work or starve.
—British Lord Sydney, on the plan for Australian convicts

Old Botany Bay

*I was the conscript
Sent to hell
To make in the desert
The living well;
I bore the heat,
I blazed the track—
Furrowed and bloody
Upon my back.
I split the rock;
I felled the tree:
The nation was—
Because of me!*
—Mary Gilmore in *Poetry in Australia*

World History — Geography and History Activities

Name .... Date .... Class ....

GEOGRAPHY and HISTORY Activity 25

Focus on Region

Australia's development from a "dumping ground" for British criminals to a thriving British commonwealth illustrates how the relationship between regions can evolve over time. Originally, Australia's isolated geography attracted the attention of British government officials as an ideal location to send convicts. After people from Great Britain had settled in Australia, the two regions became linked by human relationships and activities. Australia's natural resources—pastureland and gold—lured many free settlers. They established sheep ranches and cities, and they brought industrialization to their new home. These two factors—human (migration) and physical (resources)—created strong ties between these distant regions.

1. What two types of factors lead to a relationship between regions?

_____

2. How did the British government originally use Australia? Why?

_____

_____

3. What factors caused people's attitudes about Australia to change?

_____

4. Reread the poem "Old Botany Bay." Explain its meaning in your own words.

_____

_____

Critical Thinking

5. Demonstrating Reasoned Judgment British government officials who sent convicts to Australia didn't know anything about the land. What does this say about the British attitude toward the lawbreakers? Do you agree or disagree with this attitude?

_____

_____

6. Determining Cause and Effect How do you think their country's past as a convict colony affects the way Australians see themselves today? How do you think it affects their relationship with British people?

_____

_____

Activity

7. The United States had its beginning as a group of British colonies. Compare the relationship between the United States and Great Britain with the relationship between Australia and Great Britain.

Name _____ Date _____ Class _____

GEOGRAPHY and HISTORY Activity 26

Place: *Russia*

One summer day in Russia early in the 1800s, a young Anglo-Irish woman, Catherine Wilmot, sat writing a letter. Outside her window, serfs were mowing a field. To her, the sight of those men and women at work demonstrated that Russia was a happy place. Did events in Russia during the 1800s prove her correct?

"All the Men," Wilmot wrote of the serfs, "are clothed in white linnen Jacket & trowsers. . . . The effect is excessively picturesque, and those who imagine the Russ peasantry sunk in sloth & misery imagine a strange falsehood." She went on to contrast the typical Irish peasant to the Russian serf by asking the questions, "Have they enough to eat, to drink?" and "Have they Houses, firing [firewood] & a bed to lie on?" "Trust me," she concluded, "the Bears [Russians] would triumph, oh beyond comparison."

Yet other observers felt exactly the opposite. A Russian radical and journalist named Alexander Herzen, who lived much of his adult life in Europe, also compared Russia and the West—and found Russia seriously wanting. Each observer described the same place using a different standard.

The Individual in Russia

Even in the worst periods of European history, we encounter some respect for the individual, some recognition of independence. . . . We [in Russia] have nothing similar. With us the individual has always been crushed, absorbed, he has never even tried to escape. Free speech with us has always been considered insolence, independence, subversion; man was engulfed in the State, dissolved in the community. . . . Were it not that Russia was so vast, that the . . . system of power was so chaotically established, so incompletely administered, one might have said without exaggeration that no human being with any sense of his own dignity could live in Russia.

—From "From the Other Shore," by Alexander Herzen (1849)

One hundred years after Catherine Wilmot wrote her letter, Russian peasants still lived simple lives. Although serfdom was abolished in Russia in 1861, much of the system of repression decried by Herzen remained in place. In his painting *The Potato Harvest*, Arkady Plastov shows Russian peasants in the early 1900s gathering potatoes as their ancestors had done centuries earlier.

Name .... Date .... Class ....

GEOGRAPHY and HISTORY Activity 26

Focus on Place

Any description of a place reflects the values, attitudes, and perceptions of the person giving that description. In judging the accuracy of place description, it is necessary to take into account the background of the person making it.

In fact, a place description often tells as much about the describer as the place described. Catherine Wilmot's description of Russian serfs reveals her belief that material things—food, shelter, and fuel—are enough to keep people happy. It also suggests that she feels lower social classes should be content with less than she has. But Alexander Herzen does not mention material happiness. For him, the only true measure of a society is the freedom it grants its members, whether peasants or aristocrats.

1. What should you take into account when hearing someone's description of a place?

2. Why did Wilmot's opinion of the lives of serfs in Russia differ from that of Herzen's?

3. Both Wilmot and Herzen compare Russia to other lands. How does their choice of comparison reflect their biases?

4. Both Wilmot and Herzen were from families of high social rank. How would you have expected this to affect their views?

Critical Thinking

5. **Making Inferences** List one or more of your own attitudes that determine your reaction to the painting on the previous page.

6. **Synthesizing Information** The Russian novelist Ivan Turgenev wrote to Herzen in 1862, mocking his belief that the Russian peasant would become a force for change in society. Do you think the Russian peasant was opposed to change in society? Why or why not?

Activity

7. Clip stories about Russia from a newspaper for a period of about two weeks. Then write an essay in answer to the following question, using the clippings as evidence to support your response: Is Herzen's description of Russia still valid today?

GEOGRAPHY and HISTORY Activity 27

Movement: *Railroads in India*

Indian writer Rabindranath Tagore published a short story in 1898 about a man named Pramathanath, who visits Great Britain and returns to his native India proudly wearing European clothes. After seeing the British insult his fellow Indians on a new train, however, Pramathanath angrily throws his clothes into a blazing fire. How did British rule in India create conflicts for Indians?

The bloody Sepoy Rebellion of 1857 had a lasting impact on British-Indian relations. The British living in India built whites-only towns that could be easily defended in case of future revolts. Many Indians, on the other hand, sought to improve their lives through education. Some attended colleges in Great Britain, where they perfected their English, studied law, and witnessed democracy at work.

India changed rapidly after the Sepoy Rebellion. British companies built thousands of miles of railroads, dug dozens of coal mines, and started huge coffee and tea plantations. Yet the profits from these new ventures rarely trickled down to the Indian people, and the economic and social gap between the British and the Indians grew wider with each passing year. Meanwhile, the gaps between Indians began narrowing. The railroads brought them closer to each other, as did their use of a new common language—English.

Pulled Between Two Cultures

On the return journey, a European Sergeant of the Police expelled some Indian gentlemen from a railway-carriage with great insolence. Pramathanath, dressed in his European clothes, was there. He, too, was getting out, when the Sergeant said: "You needn't move, sir. Keep your seat, please."

At first Pramathanath felt flattered at the special respect thus shown to him. When, however, the train went on, the dull rays of the setting sun, at the west of the fields, now ploughed up and stripped of green, seemed in his eyes to spread a glow of shame over the whole country. Sitting near the window of his lonely compartment, he seemed to catch a glimpse of the downcast eyes of his Motherland, hidden behind the trees. As Pramathanath sat there, lost in reverie, burning tears flowed down his cheeks, and his heart burst with indignation.

— From "We Crown Thee King" by Rabindranath Tagore

This locomotive overturned as Indian laborers were laying tracks, in about 1880. India's vast and rugged terrain presented many problems for train crews. However, as they tied the country together, railroads helped transport India into the modern age. India had only 432 miles of railroad track in 1859; by 1899, it had 25,000 miles of track.

Name _____ Date _____ Class _____

GEOGRAPHY and HISTORY Activity 27

Focus on Movement

The new railroads made it easier for the British to transport goods across India. Communities that had once been isolated were now connected by a vast web of steel rails. Connections between the Indian people also grew stronger. Before the British arrived, Indians in different parts of the country spoke hundreds of different languages, making communication difficult. Now the new railroads and the new common language—English—helped Indians work together toward a common goal: reclaiming their homeland for themselves. India in the late 1800s provides just one example of how improvements in transportation and communication can lead to profound cultural changes. In the case of Pramathanath, the improvements also prompted a change in attitude.

1. What purpose did the British have for building railroads in India?
   _____

2. What effects did the railroads have on Indian culture beyond their original purpose?
   _____

3. What effects did the English language have on Indian culture?
   _____

4. What was Pramathanath's attitude toward British culture when he boarded the train? Give evidence to support your answer.
   _____

5. Why did Pramathanath's attitude change?
   _____

Critical Thinking

6. **Drawing Conclusions** Do you think it was wise of the British to improve transportation and communication systems in India? Explain your answer.
   _____
   _____

7. **Predicting Consequences** What improvements in transportation and communication are occurring in your society? What long-term effects do you think these improvements will have?
   _____
   _____

Activity

8. Debate the following statement with your classmates: By improving communication, television has benefited modern society. Present evidence to support your position.

GEOGRAPHY and HISTORY Activity 28

Human-Environment Interaction: *The Battle of the Somme*

Where there had once been green forests and groves, there was now only the occasional leafless, branchless tree. Autumn had come to the Somme valley of France in 1916. But it was an artificial autumn, brought on by bombs, bullets, and hand grenades. How did advances in military technology change the nature of warfare with the outbreak of World War I?

Before World War I, vacationing Parisians used to flock north to the Somme River. The waterway flowed lazily through a gentle countryside dotted with rich farms, quaint villages, and thickly wooded hills. Happy to escape the stresses of city life, the Parisians swam in the Somme, strolled through the woods, and nibbled on bread and cheese from the local bakeries and farms.

The tourists barely dented the local food supply. For hundreds of years, the rolling plains around the Somme had been one of France's leading agricultural regions. Wheat, barley, oats, sugar beets, and all manner of fruits and vegetables grew in the area's fertile soil. Farmers raised cattle by the thousands and produced cheese and butter by the ton.

When the opposing armies arrived at the Somme in 1916, they dug trenches instead of seed rows. Their constant artillery fire soon destroyed the land between the trenches, turning it into a desolate landscape known as No Man's Land. It was No Tree's Land as well, because nothing could stand up to the powerful artillery shells.

A Desolate Landscape

I reached a [crossroads] where four lanes broadened into a confused patch of destruction. Fallen trees, shell holes, a hurriedly dug trench beginning and ending in an uncertain manner, abandoned rifles, broken branches with their sagging leaves, an unopened box of ammunition, sandbags half-filled with bombs, a derelict machine-gun propping up the head of an immobile figure in uniform, with a belt of ammunition drooping from the breech into a pile of red-stained earth—this is the livery of War. Shells were falling, over and short, near and wide, to show that somewhere over the hill a gunner was playing the part of blind fate for all who walked past this well-marked spot. Here, in the struggle between bursting iron and growing timber, iron had triumphed....
—From *Up To Mametz*,
  by L. W. Griffith (1923)

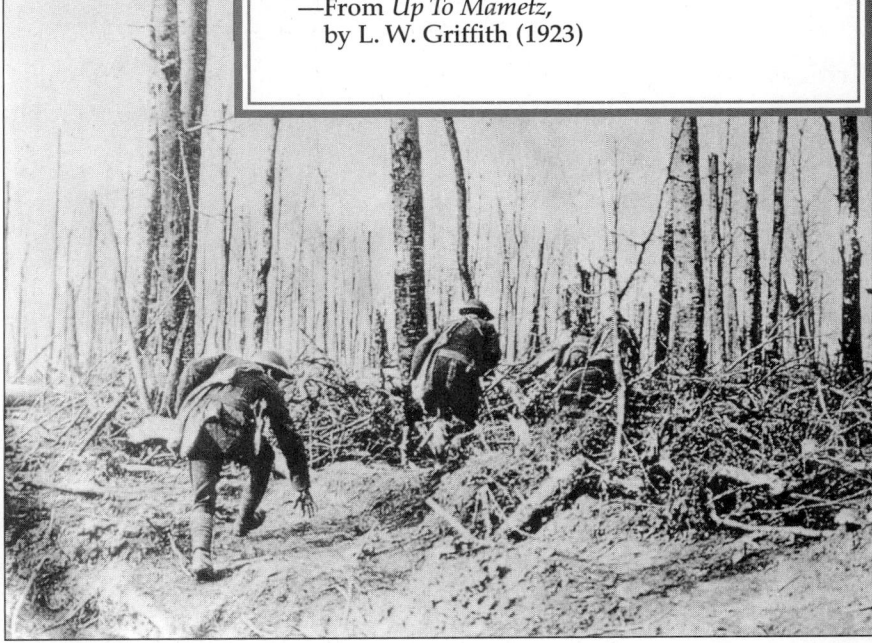

"Over the top!" resounded along Allied lines as soldiers poured from their trenches into No Man's Land. The scarred remains of a forest show the devastating effects of trench warfare on the countryside near the Somme River.

World History

GEOGRAPHY and HISTORY Activity 28

Focus on Human-Environment Interaction

Different groups of people interact with their environment in different ways. The farmers of the Somme, for example, grew wheat, oats, and vegetables in the fertile soil of the plains, but they grew few crops on the surrounding hills. It was difficult for them to clear the trees from the hills and plant crops on the hillsides. Besides, the soil was richer on the plains.

The soldiers had a different opinion of the Somme's geographic features. They prized the hills and dreaded the plains. The hills gave commanding views across a wide area and were easy to defend. The plains, on the other hand, offered little protection and exposed soldiers to attack from all sides.

1. Why did soldiers and farmers have different opinions of the Somme's geographic features?

2. Which features of the Somme were important to farmers? Why?

3. Which features were important to soldiers? Why?

4. Compare the impacts of farming and warfare on the Somme.

5. What impact do you think a modern war would have on the Somme? Why?

Critical Thinking

6. **Evaluating Information** Which aspects of the Somme's geography might interest a modern factory owner? Why?

7. **Demonstrating Reasoned Judgement** In what sense were the opposing sides in World War I transforming geography when they created No Man's Land?

Activity

8. Do you think the land of the Somme ever returned to its prewar condition? Working with a group, research the Somme or another famous World War I battlefield. Try to answer the following questions: Which parts of the land were able to recover? How long did the recovery take? Which parts were unable to recover? Why? Report your findings to the class.

GEOGRAPHY and HISTORY Activity 29

Location: *Jews in Europe*

On April 1, 1933, German soldiers in full uniform stood at the entrances of certain department stores and other shops, urging customers not to enter. "This is a Jewish business!" the soldiers shouted. "Remember to boycott the Jews!" Few customers dared to enter and few Jewish stores remained open. That day marked the beginning of Germany's official persecution of the Jews. Why did the German government initiate a policy of persecuting its own citizens?

In Berlin's Jewish Ghetto

The entrance to the Wassertorstrasse was a big stone archway, a bit of old Berlin, daubed with hammers and sickles and Nazi crosses and plastered with tattered bills which advertised auctions or crimes. It was a deep shabby cobbled street, littered with sprawling children's tears....

Down in the murky pit of the courtyard, where the fog, in this clammy autumn weather, never lifted, the street singers and musicians succeeded each other in a performance which was nearly continuous. There were parties of boys with mandolins, an old man who played the concertina, and a father who sang with his little girls....

Another regular visitor was the Jewish tailor and outfitter, who sold clothes of all kinds on the installment plan. He was small and gentle and very persuasive. All day long he made his rounds of the tenements in the district, collecting fifty pfennigs here, a mark there, scratching up his precarious livelihood, like a hen, from this apparently barren soil.

—From *Goodbye to Berlin* (1935) by Christopher Isherwood

After World War I, many successful Jews moved in the upper class of European society. In Germany, for example, Jews owned steel mills, railroads, shipping lines, department stores, and banks. The lives of these wealthy Jews closely resembled those of other rich Germans.

Yet for every Jew in the upper class, there were dozens of middle and working class Jews. Beginning in the late 1800s, millions of Jews fled the impoverished villages in Russia and eastern Europe. Some traveled all the way to the United States; others crowded into ghettos in western European cities such as Berlin, where they eked out a living by toiling in sweatshops or peddling various wares. As their profits grew, they opened small shops and businesses.

German Jews, both rich and poor, seemed destined for success in the 1920s and 1930s. But a rising tide of jealousy and hatred brought a tragic end to their dreams—and, in millions of cases, to their lives.

Jewish tailors and small-business owners were often confined to the ghettos of central European cities because they were viewed as unwelcome competitors.

World History — Geography and History Activities 57

Name _____ Date _____ Class _____

GEOGRAPHY and HISTORY Activity 29

Focus on Location

Location—rural or urban, seaside or mountainside, remote or accessible—exerts a powerful influence on human activities. It can determine the kind of work people do and shape their way of living. The Jews who fled from eastern to western Europe in the late 1800s and early 1900s had to change their livelihoods. In the east they had survived primarily by farming. Because there were no farms in the western ghettos, the Jews who moved there turned to peddling and factory work. Customers were easy to find in the crowded cities, and the urban factories needed cheap labor. By adapting their lives to their new locations, the Jews were able to succeed.

1. Why is tailoring well suited to urban locations?

2. How did location influence the lives of Jews in eastern Europe?

3. How were the street musicians in Berlin like the Jewish tailor? How did they differ?

4. Why do you think many Germans felt jealousy and hatred toward the Jews?

5. Describe how location influences human activities in your community, such as jobs or recreation.

Critical Thinking

6. **Making Inferences** Do you think location plays as great a role in human activities as it did 60 years ago? Use specific examples to explain your answer.

7. **Making Comparisons** Imagine you can build a new city anywhere in the United States. Which location would you choose? Why?

Activity

8. Brainstorm with your classmates a list of innovative occupational and recreational activities that might be particularly suitable for your community's location.

Geography and History Activities

World History

Name _____ Date _____ Class _____

GEOGRAPHY and HISTORY Activity 30

Region: *East Africa*

In the summer of 1884, a British explorer in what is now Tanzania wrote: "Here is a country as large as Switzerland, enjoying a singularly fertile soil and healthy climate.... Within a few years it must be either English, French, or German." The land did in fact become German, then English, and finally Tanzanian. But to whom did this fertile land really belong?

When Julius Nyerere was born in Tanganyika (now Tanzania) in 1922, his country was a series of lines on a colonial map, dividing and combining diverse tribal groups, each with its own language and customs. Great Britain and Germany had formed both Tanganyika and neighboring Kenya when they carved up East Africa in the late 1800s.

Nyerere led his country to independence in 1961, but for him that was just a start. He realized that the map of Africa was a mere piece of paper, and he saw no reason for Africans to accept the boundaries imposed on them by European imperialists. Instead, he urged his fellow leaders to form a united Africa, the government of which would encompass the entire continent. He developed these ideas in a speech to the United Nations in December 1961. Many listened, but few acted. Africa remains deeply divided along colonial lines.

Nyerere's Independence Address

It is not possible for Tanganyika to remain an island of freedom and peace surrounded by troubled and unfreed areas. On either side of all our borders live people with a common language, and common traditions. We cannot fail to be concerned with what goes on in countries which adjoin Tanganyika, because their troubles are also our troubles.... We are anxious to join with other African States in abolishing the artificial boundaries which were imposed upon us by the colonial system.... The unity of the whole of our continent is our ambition.

—Julius Nyerere, United Nations speech, 1961

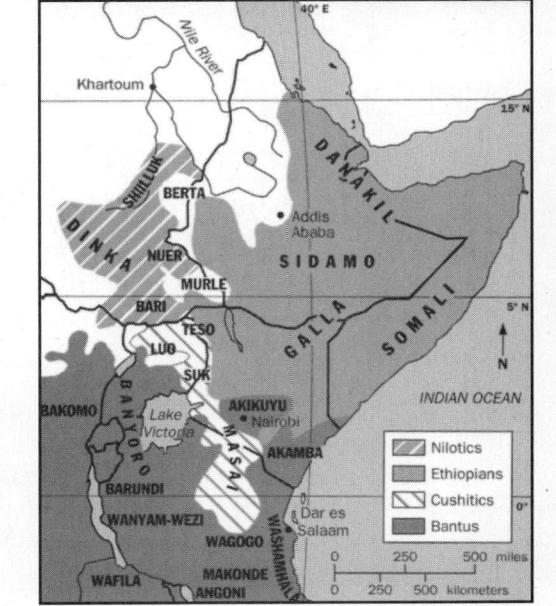

Peoples of East Africa

The political boundaries of East Africa, largely created during the colonial era, bear little relationship to tribal boundaries. Compare this map with the map of Africa shown on page A20 in your textbook. Note that the Kenya-Tanzania border splits the Masai lands in two. The Masai, who used to herd livestock freely across these lands, are now restricted in their movements. They also find themselves in conflict with the neighboring Kikuyu. These restrictions and conflicts have forced the Masai to alter their traditional nomadic ways.

World History   Geography and History Activities **59**

Name _____ Date _____ Class _____

GEOGRAPHY and HISTORY Activity 30

Focus on Region

Geographic areas may belong to more than one region. The Masai herding grounds of Tanzania, for example, belong to both the Masai tribal region and to the political region called Tanzania. The map on the previous page shows how the regions overlap.

Your community may also belong to overlapping regions. Your climatic region, for example, probably overlaps your political, economic, and vegetation regions. Other overlapping regions may include those based on population or physical features. The particular combination of regions of which your community is a part helps make it unique.

1. Why can one location belong to many regions?

2. Which regions overlap in southern Kenya?

3. Explain why political and tribal regions overlap in East Africa.

4. Based on East Africa's overlapping regions, what kinds of conflicts do you think might exist there?

5. How did Julius Nyerere propose to settle conflicts created by overlapping regions in Africa?

Critical Thinking

6. **Predicting Consequences** What do you think would happen if the map of East Africa were redrawn to reflect tribal boundaries? What problems would be solved? What problems might arise? Why?

7. **Analyzing Information** Which types of political regions overlap in your community? Do you think the overlap is helpful or harmful? Give specific examples to support your point of view.

Activity

8. Identify a local, national, or international problem that can be traced to overlapping regions. Draw a map that shows the existing regions; then draw a revised map that shows how the problem could be solved. Write a few sentences to explain your revisions.

GEOGRAPHY and HISTORY Activity 31

Movement: *The Blockade of Japan*

For ten weeks, Allied planes and submarines had dogged the Japanese supply convoy, picking off its ships until only one was left, the *Sarawak Maru*. Finally, on March 20, 1945, that tanker, too, sank in a seething cloud of fire. How did the fate of the *Sarawak Maru* foreshadow the surrender of Japan?

The war between the Allies and Japan in the Pacific was fought over immense stretches of ocean that prevented rapid movement except by air. This meant that ships traveling the long sea-lanes were vulnerable to attack.

Japan, as a nation of islands with limited natural resources, depended heavily on shipping to bring in raw materials from its overseas conquests. It imported almost all of the oil needed to fuel its war machine, along with 80 percent of the iron ore it used to build ships. Half of its food also came from outside the home islands.

Recognizing this weakness, Allied strategists targeted Japan's merchant fleet. From the pitching decks of aircraft carriers, U.S. planes led the attack on the lifelines of the Japanese war machine.

By 1944, the flow of resources was in such peril that the Japanese took a desperate measure—kamikaze, or suicide plane attacks on U.S. ships. A shortage of planes, however, undermined this strategy, and the relentless campaign against Japanese supply lines continued. Submarines, planes, and sea mines destroyed 90 percent of Japan's shipping by August 1945, and the depleted war machine faltered.

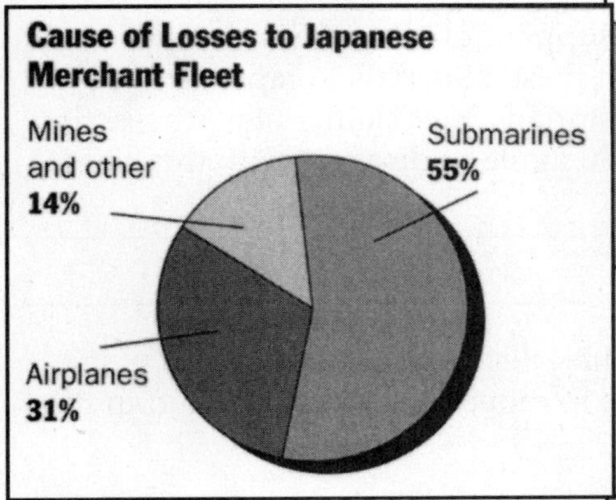

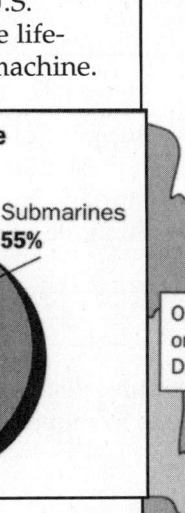

Cause of Losses to Japanese Merchant Fleet
- Mines and other: 14%
- Submarines: 55%
- Airplanes: 31%

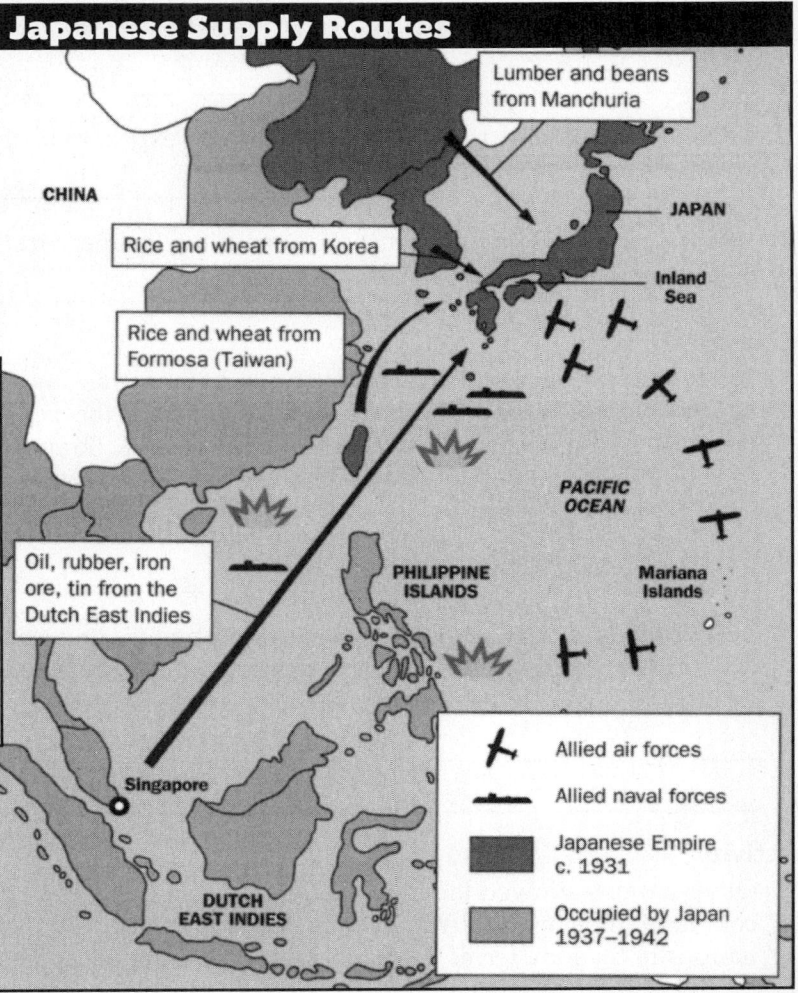

Japanese Supply Routes
- Lumber and beans from Manchuria
- Rice and wheat from Korea
- Rice and wheat from Formosa (Taiwan)
- Oil, rubber, iron ore, tin from the Dutch East Indies

Legend:
- Allied air forces
- Allied naval forces
- Japanese Empire c. 1931
- Occupied by Japan 1937–1942

Raw materials streaming toward Japan were cut off by an Allied blockade. Not only did the Allies sink ships sailing between the resource-rich Dutch East Indies and Japan, but Allied planes also dropped mines into the waters of Japan's vital Inland Sea, sharply curtailing movement among the home islands themselves.

World History — Geography and History Activities — 61

Geography and History Activity 31

Focus on Movement

Barriers can have a dramatic effect on the movement of people, products, and ideas. Evaluating barriers to movement can disclose an opponent's weakness during war or reveal causes and effects to historians.

Barriers are not necessarily forbidding landforms such as mountain ranges. The Japanese had to bring oil 2,500 miles (4,000 kilometers) from the Dutch East Indies to the home islands. For them, distance over open seas proved a barrier.

How readily movement takes place also depends on transportation. Japanese transportation failed when most of Japan's available ships were destroyed and it had little iron to build more.

1. Why do we need to evaluate barriers to movement?

2. What effect did the barriers of sea distances and the Allied blockade have on the Japanese war effort?

3. Which of Japan's wartime imports would you expect to be the last to be disrupted? Why?

4. What was the chief reason for the failure of the Japanese transportation system?

Critical Thinking

5. **Determining Cause and Effect** The United States was a key supplier of oil and gas to Japan before the war, but the U.S. government prohibited the sale of these materials to Japan in 1939 in response to the Japanese invasion of mainland Asia. Some historians later claimed that this action forced Japan to invade the Dutch East Indies. Explain why you agree or disagree with this claim.

6. **Evaluating Information** Unlike Germany, Japan was never subjected to a destructive land invasion by enemy troops. Explain this by evaluating barriers to movement in Europe and in the Pacific.

Activity

7. Other nations allowed Japan to set up economic barriers to protect its struggling industries from competition after World War II. Some economists believe that trade barriers are harmful to all nations in the long term. From what you know about Japan's present trade barriers against U.S. products, do you agree with this theory? Explain your answer in one paragraph.

Name .... Date .... Class ....

GEOGRAPHY and HISTORY Activity 32

Region: *The Bipolar World*

In 1963 President John F. Kennedy stood on a windswept platform outside the Brandenburg Gate of the Berlin Wall and told a cheering throng, *"Ich bin ein Berliner"* (I am a citizen of Berlin). People cheered and wept. His words became immortal. What was Kennedy trying to tell the world?

When the Berlin Wall went up in 1961, it divided families, it divided a city, and it divided a country. Symbolically, it cut the world in two as well. Berlin represented a global struggle between two political systems, communism and democracy—or, as Westerners saw it, between tyranny and freedom. As long as the wall remained, Kennedy's words implied, every free person lived in its shadow and became a "citizen" of Berlin.

The war of words that Kennedy conducted so eloquently with his counterpart, the fiery Nikita Khrushchev, was intended to win the minds of people around the world. The American President, like most Westerners, valued democracy, freedom, and a capitalist economic system—even though, as he acknowledged in his speech, "freedom has many difficulties and democracy is not perfect." Communist leaders rejected Kennedy's principles. They believed that he represented capitalist wealth and privilege, which they saw as decadent and unfair. Each side fully expected that its values would ultimately triumph, converting the world.

Communism had spread to a large area of the globe by 1963. However, that area would begin to recede in the 1980s, as the problems Kennedy noted in Berlin contributed to the downfall of Communist regimes in most countries.

At the Brandenburg Gate

Freedom has many difficulties and democracy is not perfect, but we have never had to put a wall up to keep our people in, to prevent them from leaving us. . . . [T]he wall is the most obvious and vivid demonstration of the failures of the Communist system . . . it is an offense not only against humanity, separating families, dividing husbands and wives and brothers and sisters, and dividing a people who wish to be joined together. . . . All free men, wherever they may live, are citizens of Berlin, and therefore, as a free man, I take pride in the words "Ich bin ein Berliner."

—John F. Kennedy, June 26, 1963

Geopolitical Regions 1963

Cold war flash points in the Western Hemisphere included Cuba, Nicaragua, and Chile.

The U.S. feared the spread of Communist influence in southern Asia, the Middle East, and Africa.

■ Communist Countries

Nations Under Communist Rule

Albania	East Germany	Poland
Bulgaria	Hungary	Romania
China	Mongolia	Soviet Union
Cuba	North Korea	Yugoslavia
Czechoslovakia	North Vietnam	

World History   Geography and History Activities   **63**

Name _____ Date _____ Class _____

GEOGRAPHY and HISTORY Activity 32

Focus on Region

The cold war is an example of how people's values and principles shaped world geography. The iron curtain was an imaginary political line that divided Communist and democratic nations. But it also divided the world in terms of two geographic regions, East and West. In fact, during the cold war, the interaction of politics and geography gave rise to a new term: geopolitics.

For half a century, many people saw the globe as divided into these two geopolitical regions. Some countries, however, rejected this bipolar, or two-sided, view of the world. They noted the existence of a "third world" of non-aligned countries whose values and goals differed from those of the superpowers. Later, this idea of three world regions—two powerful regions, East and West, and a weaker class of developing nations—faded as well. Countries such as Japan, once a part of this so-called third world, became economic giants. Meanwhile, a decline in the East bloc weakened that region's influence. The world's geopolitical regions may shift in future years, as countries develop and their values and alliances change.

1. What are geopolitical regions?
   _____

2. How did people's values during the cold war help to create a bipolar view of the world?
   _____

3. How did the idea of a third region come about?
   _____

4. What does the map tell you about the geopolitical regions that existed in 1963?
   _____

Critical Thinking

5. **Recognizing Ideologies** Pick a foreign country and describe how your values shape your perception of that country.
   _____

6. **Analyzing Information** The Berlin Wall was intended to stop the flow of people to the West and the flow of Western ideas to the East. How successful do you think it was in achieving each of these goals?
   _____

Activity

7. Imagine that you have been asked to present a proposal for creating a "United States of Europe" to various European leaders. Working with a group of classmates, draw a map showing what the new country might look like. Specify the location of the capital city, the number of states, and the borders of these states. Prepare arguments supporting the formation of the new country. Present your final map and arguments to the class.

GEOGRAPHY and HISTORY Activity 33

Place: *Hong Kong*

Hong Kong is a place of extremes. Along the dramatic slopes of Victoria Peak, opulent mansions overlook the South China Sea. Elsewhere, in the densely packed slums of Kowloon, people rent "cage apartments"—stacked wire cages the size of coffins. In 1997 Hong Kong, a former British colony for more than a century, became a part of Communist-ruled China while keeping its capitalist system.

Located on the southeastern coast of China, Hong Kong is formed by more than 235 islands and a small peninsula connected to mainland China. Hong Kong is one of the most crowded places in the world, with as many as 68,500 people per square mile in the urban centers.

Although Hong Kong has been settled since ancient times, the Chinese territory of Hong Kong is unique because it was under British rule for many years. However, unlike other colonies, Hong Kong never fully surrendered to the British, who sought to use its ports to control trade in southern Asia. Rather, in 1898 the government of China "leased" part of mainland Hong Kong to Great Britain for a period of 99 years. During those years, Britain ruled Hong Kong as a dependency, making it one of the most important ports in Asia and an international center of finance, commerce, and tourism. In 1984 Great Britain agreed to relinquish the colony. The transfer, which took place in 1997, placed one of the world's most successful capitalist economies in the hands of China's Communist regime. Ironically, many people in Hong Kong had moved there to escape communism.

Under its 1984 agreement with Great Britain, China promised to maintain Hong Kong's capitalist system for 50 years after 1997. But many people did not wait to find out if the Chinese would keep their promise of "one country, two systems." Companies relocated, and hundreds of thousands of people emigrated to Australia, Canada, and the United States. One way or the other, Hong Kong today is destined for radical change.

"[Most people who settled in Hong Kong] were exiles. They never regarded Hong Kong as their home. They formed what they called sojourners societies, groups from Shanghai or Wuhan or wherever they had come from. The first time the census showed that a majority of people in Hong Kong had actually been born here was in 1971, and they were mostly children. Only now do we have a majority of people, like me, who were born and grew up here and have a stake in the place."

—Frank Ching, author and journalist

World History — Geography and History Activities — 65

Name _____ Date _____ Class _____

GEOGRAPHY and HISTORY Activity 33

Focus on Place

Very few places on the earth remain untouched by humans. So when you visit a place, you're seeing, in effect, a physical record of the activities, values, and history of the people who have passed through it. The characteristics of place unique to Hong Kong include the mixing of British and Asian culture and the history of free trade under British rule.

Just as people influence a place, the physical geography of a place influences its population. Hong Kong's location and deep-water ports have attracted traders and businesspeople and encouraged the dense distribution of people along its seacoast.

1. List three main characteristics of Hong Kong.
   _____

2. How has Hong Kong's physical geography affected the occupations of its people?
   _____

3. How have people affected the physical geography of Hong Kong?
   _____

4. Since 1997, Hong Kong has been part of China. How is the history and economy of Hong Kong different from that of other parts of China?
   _____
   _____

Critical Thinking

5. **Recognizing Bias** Many Hong Kong citizens fear the effects of Chinese rule. What do you think they fear?
   _____
   _____

6. **Drawing Conclusions** From 1976 to 1988, 100,000 Vietnamese boat people fled to Hong Kong, forcing the colony to impose limits on the influx. What do you think made Hong Kong a major destination for Vietnamese refugees? How do you think the migration has changed Hong Kong?
   _____
   _____

Activity

7. Certain that Chinese rule would bring disaster, some people in Hong Kong suggested desperate measures. One idea was to relocate the entire territory—perhaps renting the northern tip of Australia. Write a one-page essay giving imaginative answers to the following questions: Assuming people could afford to try such a venture, could they really relocate Hong Kong? Would it have the same qualities of place if it were not in the same location? What effect would a new location have on the population of New Hong Kong?

Name _____ Date _____ Class _____

GEOGRAPHY and HISTORY Activity 34

Movement: *South African Apartheid*

Freedom of movement is a privilege that most people take for granted. We assume it is our basic right to live where we want and to travel where we desire. However, the government policy of apartheid—a system that dominated South Africa from early settlement until the 1990s—placed great restrictions on where people could move within the country.

The population of South Africa includes many races, which were kept strictly segregated under the system of apartheid. Most of the white population is composed of Afrikaners, or settlers of Dutch descent. People of color generally fall into three groups: the Bantu are black Africans of either San and Khoikhoi descent; the so-called colored group includes people of mixed-race ancestry; and the third group includes those of Asian (Indian) descent.

Under the system of apartheid, racial groups were to be strictly segregated—economically, politically, socially, and geographically. The Group Areas Act of 1950 was one of many pieces of legislation designed to limit where each group was allowed to live. For example, the Bantu who wanted to move from rural areas to urban centers were restricted to special segregated areas, and they had to obtain government approval to live even there.

Beginning in the 1970s, the white minority government attempted to solidify their control even further by creating "black homelands." These were actually restricted tribal areas in which one African ethnic group would dominate. The homelands encompassed only about 12 percent of South Africa's land but held more than one-third of its population. The Bantu were to be restricted to their "homeland" and could enter a white area only with a government-issued pass.

> *I remember a period in the early 1960s, when there was a great deal of political tension, and we often used to encounter armed police in Soweto. . . . I remember the humiliation to which my parents were subjected by whites in shops and in other places where we encountered them, and the poverty. All these things had their influence on my young mind . . . and by the time I went to Orlando West High School, I was already beginning to question the injustice of the society . . . and to ask why nothing was being done to change it.*
> —Mosima Gabriel Sexwale, 1978

> *Factors such as South Africa's changing demography, the rate of urbanisation, the striving of the majority of people for a place in the sun, make it impossible . . . for the anachronistic viewpoint of the right wing and sections of the government to survive.*
> —Van Zyl Slabbert, 1988

Population of South Africa as defined by apartheid-era racial classifications

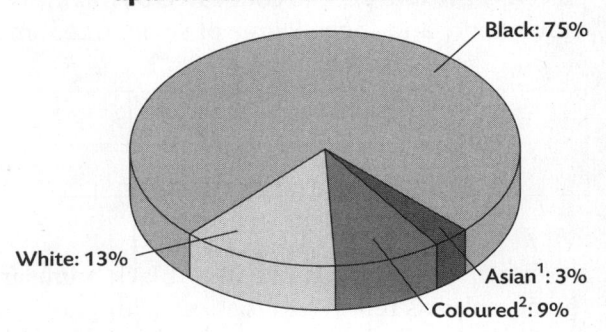

- Black: 75%
- White: 13%
- Asian[1]: 3%
- Coloured[2]: 9%

[1] Almost all citizens in this category are of Indian descent.
[2] Citizens of mixed race

World History — Geography and History Activities **67**

Name _____ Date _____ Class _____

GEOGRAPHY and HISTORY Activity 34

Focus on Movement

The white minority government of South Africa restricted the movements of the Bantu and kept cultures apart. This enforced separation resulted in many violent episodes. In 1977 civil unrest led to severely repressive actions by the police and the death of the student leader Stephen Biko. In 1984 a new South African constitution was passed that denied the Bantu political representation except in the black homelands. This legislation reinforced the restrictions on movements of the Bantu. By the late 1980s, economic pressure from the United States and the European Community had started to take effect on the government of South Africa. By 1991 most of the legal foundation of apartheid had been dismantled, and the first multiracial elections were held in South Africa in 1994. The black homelands and restrictions on movement were subsequently abolished by the parliament of South Africa.

1. How was the severe restriction of Bantu movement within South Africa consistent with the government policy of apartheid?
_____
_____

2. Why was control of the movement of the Bantu important to the continuation of apartheid?
_____
_____

Critical Thinking

3. **Drawing Conclusions** Would it have been possible for the government of South Africa to control the movement of the Bantu population indefinitely? Why or why not?
_____
_____
_____

4. **Demonstrating Reasoned Judgment** Think of other situations in which restrictions have been placed on where people could live or travel. What is the relationship between people's ability to move freely and their degree of social freedom?
_____
_____
_____

Activity

5. Research what life was like in a "black homeland" in South Africa. Use maps to show the size of the homelands relative to the rest of the Republic of South Africa. Write a brief report describing conditions in the homelands as compared to life in white South Africa.

Name .... Date .... Class ....

GEOGRAPHY and HISTORY Activity 35

Human-Environment Interaction: *Disaster in Kuwait*

The once-white robes of Saudi Arabian children turned an oily gray, as did the fur of stray cats and sheep in the fields. More than a thousand miles away, skiers in Pakistan reported black snow. Towns in Kuwait were plunged into a poisonous darkness that turned noontime into midnight. What events led to this 1991 ecological disaster in the Persian Gulf?

Defeated in war and determined to get revenge, Iraqi leader Saddam Hussein ordered his retreating army to blow up the oil wells in Kuwait, one of the world's top petroleum producers. The explosions set 550 oil wells ablaze, belching 400-foot columns of fire into the air. The inferno, extinguished after eight months, burned up 6 million barrels of oil—one-tenth of the world's daily oil consumption—every day.

The oil fires were the biggest acts of environmental terrorism in history. The wells became giant blowtorches, with temperatures of 4,000 degrees Fahrenheit that turned the surrounding sands into liquid glass. Huge pools of leaking oil threatened Kuwait's groundwater supplies and gave off highly toxic gas. Thick smoke—100,000 tons a day of airborne oil, ash, and gases—blanketed Kuwait and quickly spread to neighboring countries. The air pollution generated daily was 10 times that of all U.S. industrial emissions. As the chart below shows, the disaster threatened

A Historic Tragedy

This is the most intense burning source, probably, in the history of the world.
—Joel S. Levine, expert on biomass burning at NASA

Fires send 100,000 tons of smoke a day—including airborne oil molecules and poisonous gases such as carbon dioxide—into the atmosphere.

Dense clouds of smog hang in the atmosphere, blocking the sun and lowering temperatures.

Some particles mix with moisture in the atmosphere and fall to earth as black, oily rain and as acid rain, contaminating livestock, crops, and water supplies.

Drifting smoke threatens to spread cancer and respiratory diseases, affect temperatures on several continents, disrupt Asian monsoons upon which crops depend, and increase global warming.

Scientists disagree about how much damage the fires caused. The heavy smoke may have lowered regional temperatures in the short term. Over the long term, however, the fires may have increased global carbon dioxide emissions by as much as 5 percent, adding to global warming—the greenhouse effect.

Name _____ Date _____ Class _____

GEOGRAPHY and HISTORY Activity 35

Focus on Human-Environment Interaction

When people tally the effects of war, they usually count the dead and wounded. But war is also one of the prime examples of how humans can negatively affect their environment. In addition, we cannot predict how long it will take the environment to heal itself. The Libyan Desert, for example, is still recovering from World War II, as is Israel's Negev from wars in 1967 and 1973. It may take hundreds of years for the Gulf region to recover from the 100-hour war in 1991. One million soldiers came to the deserts of Saudi Arabia and Kuwait, bringing tanks and machinery that compacted the desert soil and toxic fuels that poisoned the sands. The U.S.-led coalition forces alone dropped 88,500 tons of explosives on the desert. The region's delicate ecosystem may turn out to be a huge casualty of the war.

1. What short-term damage occurred from the fires?

_____

_____

2. Why is it difficult for scientists to assess the level of long-term environmental damage from disasters such as the Kuwaiti oil fires?

_____

3. During the war, Iraq also dumped billions of barrels of Kuwaiti oil into the Persian Gulf. Name two likely consequences of that action.

_____

_____

Critical Thinking

4. **Recognizing Bias** Why do you think the environmental effects of war are sometimes overlooked?

_____

_____

5. **Drawing Conclusions** Name three other historical examples of the negative effects of humans on environment. Then list three positive effects.

_____

_____

Activity

6. On a world map, locate Kuwait. Then trace the following course: Start in Romania. Move south through Egypt and the Sudan, then east through the Horn of Africa at Somalia. Cross the Arabian Sea to Bombay, India. Cut northeast through India to the Himalayas. Follow the mountains northwest and cross the southern plains of the former Soviet Union to the Caspian Sea. Go west to the Black Sea and return to your starting point. The enclosed area is the region most directly affected by the Kuwaiti oil fires. The long-term effects, however, could be felt worldwide.

GEOGRAPHY and HISTORY Activity 36

Movement: *Mexico City*

In Mexico City they are called *paracaidistas*—parachutists—because they seem to come out of nowhere. They are squatters, arriving at the rate of more than 1,000 a day. An encampment of *paracaidistas* can appear literally overnight, as they descend swiftly upon an empty plot of land and set up ramshackle shelters in the darkness. Where do these people come from?

The *paracaidistas* and others who pour into Mexico City at an alarming rate are campesinos, impoverished rural peasants seeking jobs and housing in the Mexican capital. They come despite the grim realities of life in this crowded city: It already houses almost one-fourth of the nation's population; in 30 percent of the families living in Mexico City, the entire family (averaging five people) sleeps in one room; housing conditions are so poor that families have taken up residence in city dumps, living in caves of garbage and paying "rent" to the self-appointed landlords of the dumps.

The vast shantytowns that encircle the nation's capital are called the "lost cities"; they lack roads, sewers, and schools. People there live in severe poverty—not as severe, however, as conditions in the countryside. In addition, many people follow relatives and friends to the city, and young people are drawn by the stories of exciting city life. As the bar graph shows, the flow of migrants from the countryside shows no signs of ebbing.

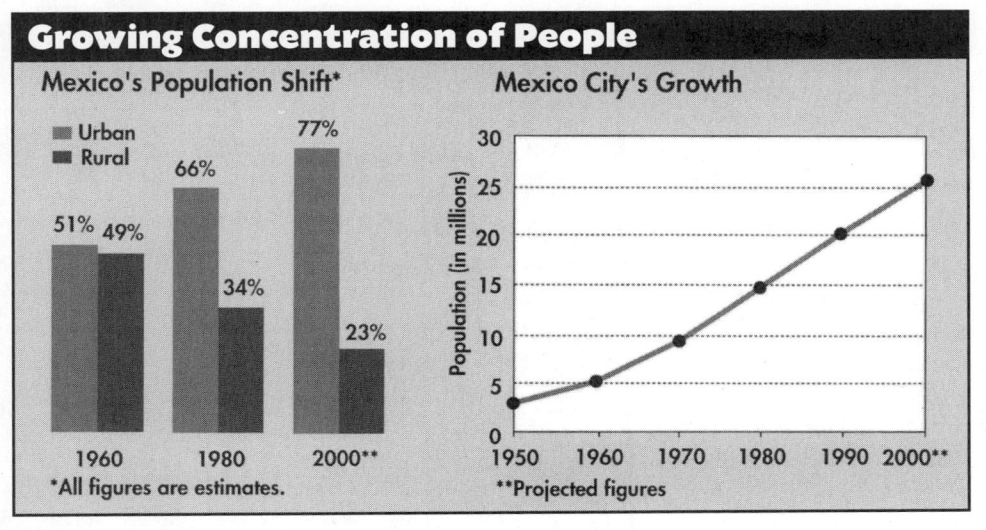

> ### Why Come to Mexico City?
> *My military service brought me here first. Later my cousin Margarita got a job as a cook in a private home, and she got me a job as the gardener. . . . [N]ow I have worked three years in electric repairs with a friend.*
> —José Ruiz, a farmboy from Oaxaca

Growing Concentration of People

Mexico's Population Shift*

Year	Urban	Rural
1960	51%	49%
1980	66%	34%
2000**	77%	23%

*All figures are estimates.

Mexico City's Growth (Population in millions)

Year	Population
1950	~3
1960	~5
1970	~9.5
1980	~15
1990	~20
2000**	~26

**Projected figures

Mexico was a largely rural country for hundreds of years, but by 1960 it had become predominantly urban; by 2020 it will become overwhelmingly so, as the bar graph shows. Most of the people moving to the cities are in fact moving to one city, Mexico City, which, as the line graph shows, is expected to continue its extraordinary growth in the next century.

Name .... Date .... Class ....

GEOGRAPHY and HISTORY Activity 36

Focus on Movement

People migrate for many reasons. Geographers refer to a "push-pull" effect that causes people to move from place to place. In the case of Mexico, the "push" is this: Jobs are scarce in rural areas, due to the rapidly growing campesino population. Out-of-work farmers simply cannot afford to feed their families and are forced to move.

Mexico City exerts a "pull" effect: It is the source of about one-third of the country's factory and commercial jobs; two-thirds of the nation's bureaucracy is located there; it is the nation's capital as well. It is as if Los Angeles, New York, and Washington, D.C. were all in the same place. *Paracaidistas* lured to the city can get clear title to public land after squatting for five years. Transplanted rural people raise vegetables and chickens on the roofs and porches of their new city homes.

1. In geography, what is the "push-pull" effect?

2. How are the two graphs on the previous page related? What do they reveal?

3. Besides jobs, what factors account for the "pull" effect—the lure—of Mexico City?

Critical Thinking

4. **Expressing Problems Clearly** Mexico City is an unlikely place for the world's second-largest city. It is farther away from a major water source than any other city, and it is ringed by mountains that trap air pollution, causing the world's thickest smog. What effect do you think rural migration has had on the city's water and smog problems? List other possible effects from population growth.

5. **Identifying Central Issues** Imagine that you are an economics minister in Mexico. What steps would you take to try to slow the huge migration to the capital?

6. **Making Inferences** Would you expect migration from rural to urban areas to be extensive in other Latin American countries? Explain.

Activity

7. As Mexico's cultural and governmental capital, the ancient city possesses great beauty and historical interest that draws people from all over the world. Using library resources, write a one-page sketch of Mexico City's key features of interest. Explain how the nation's indigenous and Spanish roots affect the city's culture. Identify reasons that the city, despite its massive problems, has a reputation for being vibrant and attractive.

GEOGRAPHY and HISTORY Activity 37

Human-Environment Interaction: *Forests on Fire*

Thick smoke rises above the sky-high trees, and fire sweeps from branch to branch. Eagles, owls, and parrots scatter into the fire's searing winds. Confused animals try to flee the advancing wall of flame, but many die. Centuries of growth vanish in moments. Why are the world's rain forests going up in smoke?

Worldwide, the human appetite for land and wood is devouring nearly 1.7 acres of precious rain forest per second. At that rate, New York's Central Park would be consumed in about 12 minutes.

The Amazon rain forest of Brazil is probably the best-known rain forest. Although this area has received the most attention, scientists have estimated that Asia and Africa are losing their rain forests at a greater rate. Côte d'Ivoire (Ivory Coast), in western Africa, has lost about 90 percent of its rain forest already. And this loss is permanent—the rain forest ecosystem is complex and cannot simply be replanted.

The cause, in part, is overpopulation, which presses desperate peasants farther into the world's forests to try to make a living and feed their families. Burning clears the land quickly. The ash makes good fertilizer for a few years, and cows graze on the new young growth. But within 10 years, the soil is depleted and the land is useless desert. International aid agencies encouraged the trend during the 1970s and 1980s by funding farm programs and building new roads into the wilderness. Today, ecologists such as Willem Groeneveld help slash-and-burn farmers find better ways to live. Groeneveld convinced Brazilians to save trees by raising bees, a more profitable and less damaging enterprise. Environmentalists everywhere are looking for ways to help humans sustain themselves without destroying the trees on which future generations depend.

Saving Trees—and People

I'm not in favor of putting up a fence around [the rain forest] and throwing away the key. I am a tropical-forest ecologist. I want to save as much of the Amazon as possible, but I want the people living here to get a fair deal out of it.

—Ecologist Willem Groeneveld

Percent of Original Rain Forest Remaining

Country	by late 1980s	by 2010*
Bolivia	66	33
Brazil	76	42
Cameroon	75	56
Central America	18	5
Colombia	33	14
Congo	90	76
Ecuador	43	9
Gabon	83	79
India	11	6
Indonesia	57	38
Ivory Coast	10	0
Madagascar	32	0
Malaysia	51	20
Mexico	12	6
Myanmar	49	17
Nigeria	42	0
Peru	74	64
Thailand	17	0
Venezuela	83	76
Vietnam	23	0

* projection based on current rate of deforestation

Before the influence of humans, rain forests covered about one fourth of the earth's surface. Today they make up less than one-eighth. In many Asian and African countries, there is little woodland left to deforest.

Name _____ Date _____ Class _____

GEOGRAPHY and HISTORY Activity 37

Focus on Human-Environment Interaction

Why should students in Oregon or Texas care about the forests of Brazil? As our ability to alter the earth's environment has increased, scientists have come to understand more clearly how changes in one region can affect global systems such as weather patterns, ocean biology, and the food chain.

The survival of everyone depends on the rain forests. The plants of the rain forest give off large amounts of oxygen. They also absorb carbon dioxide, one of the gases that contribute to the greenhouse effect and global warming. In addition, the rain forests are home to a great variety of living things. Destroying rain forests reduces this biodiversity.

1. What are global environmental systems and why are people concerned about them?

2. Where is the most rapid deforestation occurring?

3. Many efforts to save the rain forests have focused on arresting people who cut down trees. How does Groeneveld's strategy differ?

4. Why does human life depend on rain forests?

Critical Thinking

5. **Analyzing Information** In the 1980s alone, there were so many new discoveries of insect life in the previously unexplored rain forests that scientists revised their estimates of the number of insect species in the world, up from about 1 million to a staggering 30 million species. What does this tell us about the earth's ecosystem?

6. **Identifying Alternatives** The tropical Isthmus of Panama is becoming a desert. In 1850, 92 percent of the country was forested; in 1986, only 37 percent. What steps could the nation take to stop the deforestation by farming campesinos?

Activity

7. A single tree in the rain forest may be home to more than 50 species of ants and more than 10,000 species of other insects. On one acre of rain forest, there may be up to 200 species of trees. And one forest canopy—the upper layer of foliage that is home to insects, birds, and animals—may contain half of all species on the earth. Considering these facts, explain in a short essay how the disruption of the rain forest could affect plant and animal life around the world.

ANSWERS

Geography and History Activity 1, pp. 1–2

1. *Students may mention survival, protecting against dangers, and controlling crucial resources such as water.*
2. The Sumerians probably lacked stones with which to build walls but found an abundance of mud in their river-valley environment.
3. A king like Gilgamesh had the political authority to direct a massive public works project. Sumerian technology included brickmaking and drainage systems.
4. They maintained two harbors. They devoted the center of their city to building a temple area.
5. *Possible answers:* Supplying the city population with its basic needs may have resulted in intensive cropping and grazing of the land and removal of all possible fuel for cooking fires. Garbage and waste disposal must have been serious problems. Contagious diseases probably spread very easily.
6. Nomads mostly relied on finding good pasture land for their food supply, whereas farmers needed the fertile soil and abundant water of the river valleys for their grain crops. Nomadic peoples were less likely than farmers to build permanent structures.
7. *Answers will vary.* Problems in urban planning include public safety, drinking water, sewage and waste disposal, and mass transportation. Students might contrast the problems of a Sumerian city of 20,000 with those of a modern city of more than 1 million inhabitants.

Geography and History Activity 2, pp. 3–4

1. its coordinates on a map grid—a pair of numbers for degrees of latitude and longitude
2. 39°N, 117.5°E
3. 34°N, 120°E
4. major floods across the North China Plain
5. loss of reliable water supplies for agriculture and drinking, and subsequent decline of population at settlements no longer near the river
6. because of the river's history of destroying villages and killing people when it floods
7. Headwaters (Lake Itasca, Minnesota): 47°N, 95°W; delta: 29°N, 89°W; sample river ports: Minneapolis-St. Paul: 44°N, 93°W; St. Louis: 38°N, 90°W; Memphis: 35°N, 90°W; New Orleans: 30°N, 90°W. *Students should research the dam system for the Mississippi, including dams built on the Missouri and Ohio Rivers, and should report on levees, floodwalls, and dredging of the river channel.*

Geography and History Activity 3, pp. 5–6

1. Places can be described not only in terms of their physical characteristics but in terms of their human characteristics.
2. You would need to know how large the population was when the city was founded, how fast the population grew, how densely populated the city was, and how the people were distributed in the city.
3. *Answers should include both physical and human characteristics.*
4. *Answers might suggest the student was part of a national or global set of people of a certain age who enjoy a particular activity.*
5. *Possible answers:* The people in Carthage were too far removed from the cultural influences that changed Tyre's religious practices, or their religion reflected different relationships with their environment.
6. Cities that were able to buy grain from the Carthaginians would be able to support larger populations than those that needed to buy grain but could not. Cities within the Carthaginian trading sphere would become larger than they would have without the grain.
7. *Answers should be connected to the founding of a place.*

Geography and History Activity 4, pp. 7–8

1. the position of a particular place with respect to other places
2. in southern Europe on the Balkan Peninsula; between the Ionian and Aegean Seas in the Mediterranean region; east of Italy and west of Turkey
3. Atlantis was near enough to Greece and to Egypt to launch a military venture.
4. agriculture, social and political organization like early cities, writing system, metalworking technology
5. To the Egyptians, crossing the Mediterranean was difficult and dangerous. As transportation technology changed, people's perceptions of relative distances changed.
6. For many centuries, Europeans saw the western horizon—the Atlantic Ocean—as the edge of the world.
7. *Answers will vary. Students will likely find that people use different relative locations when describing locations. Students should provide details to support their findings.*

Geography and History Activity 5, pp. 9–10

1. to make organizing and analyzing information easier
2. because it contained areas with different climates and landforms, and people with different cultures and political structures
3. Ideas from Greece had spread to other places.
4. approximately 2,600 miles (4,183 km)
5. *Possible answer:* As traders traveled from place to place, people began to learn the traders' language.

6. *Possible answer:* As Spanish-speaking and English-speaking people interact, each language borrows words from the other.
7. The boundaries often are along natural features, such as rivers and mountain ranges.

Geography and History Activity 6, pp. 11–12

1. *Possible answers:* the people themselves, their natural resources and manufactured products, their ideas, their armies and government officials
2. The Roman roads made up a transportation network that linked all parts of the empire.
3. *Possible answers:* straight, passable in all weather, well-drained, built to last, durable under heavy loads
4. Generals could move legions around the empire quickly to where they were most needed—for example, to quell a local rebellion.
5. *Possible answer:* The Roman Empire exerted its authority from the capital city of Rome by sending out legions, messengers, and census takers along the roads and bringing back grain, gold, and slaves.
6. The Greeks routinely sailed from their mainland to Aegean and Ionian islands and to coastal locations in Italy, Asia Minor, and northern Africa. They could move trade goods, settlers of colonies, and colony-grown grain needed to feed the mainland population. Although the Roman Empire included northern Africa, Asia Minor, and the Middle East, Roman roads could reach places far from the Mediterranean coast and also provide land routes throughout continental Europe. The Romans especially needed to move soldiers and supplies quickly over land.
7. *Have students work in small groups to brainstorm lists of similarities, differences, and modern road-building problems. Encourage interested students to research modern road-building technology or civil engineering as a career.*

Geography and History Activity 7, pp. 13–14

1. The inhabitants of a place change its character through their changing social, political, and religious activities—work, recreation, government building projects, the construction of religious monuments or buildings. Older cities or towns show evidence of earlier types of human activity. Example: a railroad station building where a railroad no longer runs.
2. fishhooks
3. The people of Jenne-jeno probably traded with people from outside of West Africa for the glass beads. There was no evidence that the beads were made at the site of Jenne-jeno.
4. As the people from Jenne-jeno traded with other West Africans and later with Islamic traders, they learned about other places, ideas, and customs. Borrowing from those other cultures, the people of Jenne-jeno brought new ways of living to the city, such as methods of agriculture, techniques and styles of constructing boats or buildings, or even styles of wearing hair or jewelry.
5. Prior to the construction of the wall, Jenne-jeno may have existed as a small scattering of houses and agricultural buildings. As it grew in size and importance in the area, the town may have felt threatened by outsiders who tried to attack the town's storehouses or wealthy citizens' homes.
6. *Possible answer:* The people of Jenne-jeno may have believed that the terra-cotta statuettes had religious value—offering safety or hospitality to any who owned or displayed such figures.
7. *Students should give evidence of land-use changes such as the construction of new housing developments, new roads, or the abandonment of certain sections of a city or town. Encourage students to explain the human activities that would accompany such land-use changes.*

Geography and History Activity 8, pp. 15–16

1. Physical characteristics of a place can include climate, landforms, water forms, vegetation, and animal life.
2. India's monsoon season is characterized by a wind that changes direction twice a year. A summer, or southwest, monsoon blows from mid-May through September, bringing heavy rains from tropical oceans; the winter, or northeast, monsoon is a reverse wind that begins in October and brings cool, dry, continental air.
3. Food production in some rural areas depends on a single growing season; a delay, therefore, can result in crop failure, higher prices, and inflation. Half of India's electricity is generated by water; a delay in the monsoon can lead to power outages.
4. Monsoons affect food production, hydropower, and land erosion.
5. People in rural and urban areas depend on the timely arrival of monsoon rains for a variety of economic, social, and political reasons. Accurate forecasts could help Indians prepare for the effects of the monsoon season.
6. The monsoon season is a significant physical characteristic of life in India; Indians therefore look forward to seeing monsoon clouds and welcome the arrival of rain. However, many people in the West do not depend on this particular aspect of climatic change and may perceive rain and clouds as symbols of sadness and melancholy.
7. *Answers will vary. It may be helpful to organize the class into two teams. Have one team research the climate of different areas in the United States, while the other team researches how these differences in climate affect physical and human environments. When each team has completed its list, have volunteers from both groups make a presentation to the entire class.*

Geography and History Activity 9, pp. 17–18

1. A region is an area that has one or more common characteristics.
2. As criteria change, the boundaries of regions also change.

3. The boundaries of the region where Indo-European languages were spoken overlap boundaries among the trading regions of Persians, nomads, and Romans. This overlap indicates a relationship among their shared language characteristics and trading regions. The region of traders speaking Chinese does not overlap the others, indicating that trade is less likely to occur without language similarities among traders.
4. You would make the boundaries of trading regions and empires exactly the same, when in fact these boundaries may be different from one another.
5. *Answers may suggest that when Europe became self-sufficient in producing silk, it no longer needed to trade for Chinese silk, and trade along the route diminished.*
6. *Answers may suggest that mountain chains often coincide with the boundaries of political regions, although there will be exceptions.*
7. *Students may point out the parallels with ancient times, raising issues of the transfer of wealth from nations such as the United States to Japan, or they may suggest that redistribution of wealth among regions is not injurious in the interdependent and interrelated world today.*

Geography and History Activity 10, pp. 19–20

1. Human characteristics of a place include cultural aspects such as language, religion, political systems, economic activities, and social structures.
2. Human characteristics of Constantinople include Greek language, descendants of various peoples, Christian beliefs, banking, trade, insurance, credit services, social and economic programs for the poor, and close ties between church and state.
3. Virtually every aspect of life in Constantinople was affected by the church, including art, architecture, politics, and social issues.
4. *Answers might include:* language(s) spoken, town or city government, religious organizations, social activities, types of industry, commerce
5. Close ties between the church and state in the Byzantine Empire meant that the Christian religion was a primary force in virtually every aspect of Byzantine life; in the United States, there is legislation separating church from state, although religious convictions play a large part in many people's political decisions.
6. Differences among people can sometimes make it difficult to find common ground for understanding and cooperation. Willingness to learn from differences can enhance international relations.
7. *Explain to students that newspapers present a perspective that might differ from other media. Ask them to keep this in mind when compiling their lists.*

Geography and History Activity 11, pp. 21–22

1. It can determine the ways in which people settle, grow crops, use resources, and adapt culturally to their surroundings.
2. People must adapt in order to survive.

3. *Students might consider their own surroundings and describe how people live, noting types of shelter used, foods eaten, and social customs.*
4. Family ties ensured protection against harsh conditions and tribal competition.
5. Byzantine society adapted to its physical environment by establishing itself as a center of trade (the result of its strategic location) and influence in the eastern lands, while the bedouin culture has led a hand-to-mouth existence based on the harshness of desert life.
6. *Answers might include a description of social customs.*
7. *Answers should include a discussion of how oil, wealth, and modernization have affected life in Arab countries generally and how government efforts to integrate the bedouin have met with disagreement and resistance on all sides.*

Geography and History Activity 12, pp. 23–24

1. The availability of various resources, including food, clothing, shelter, and ways to make a living all influence the directions in which groups move.
2. Vikings sought new sources of land, wealth, and fame.
3. Other examples of movement that resulted in new networks could include trade in the Byzantine Empire, the expansion of Islam, and the Crusades.
4. Initially, the Vikings sought to increase their wealth and access to foreign goods. The combination of Viking warrior tradition and the promise of new lands led Vikings to conquer and settle foreign lands.
5. Buried treasure points to various routes and patterns of movement during a particular period.
6. It is possible that greater military strength would have been helpful to the Europeans.
7. *Students will need to do research to prepare for the debate. Encourage students to refer to their findings when debating to support their arguments.*

Geography and History Activity 13, pp. 25–26

1. Technology presents new ideas and strategies for change, which can offer opportunities for progress.
2. Technology can aid in devising solutions to problems and challenges, as was the case with cathedral-building during the Middle Ages.
3. *Examples include skyscrapers, underground transportation, interstate highways, and tunnels.*
4. Advances in agriculture, urban planning, environmental planning, and space technology may all have an impact on physical environments.
5. The significance of the Church and the Christian religion in medieval life called for splendid structures to reflect that importance.
6. *Students might compare the ability to build a very tall masonry building to building skyscrapers or underground cities.*
7. *Emphasize to students that they will have to suspend their knowledge of what is possible today and concentrate on how their community has changed over the*

World History Geography and History Activities **77**

years. You might want to arrange a visit to the local historical society, if possible, as part of their project.

Geography and History Activity 14, pp. 27–28

1. climate, soil conditions, energy and mineral resources, rivers, good natural harbors, access to distant markets or resources
2. A location might be advantageous because of its nearness to someplace else. For instance, many suburban communities do not appear to gain any geographic advantages from locations, because they depend on their proximity to major urban areas, sometimes located more than 40 or 50 miles away, for jobs or markets.
3. spices grown on the islands of the Indonesian archipelago
4. Malacca was located on a good harbor where ships were protected from storms. Because of this good harbor, merchants from around the world gathered in Malacca to trade their goods.
5. China and Japan probably had natural resources or trading empires that could economically benefit the Portuguese at that time.
6. *Possible answer:* Native populations may have learned some of the languages of the merchants who came to trade in Srivijaya in order to provide services for those traders.
7. *You may want to suggest that students read the article "Two Worlds, Time Apart: Indonesia" in* National Geographic, *vol. 175, no. 1, January 1989. Encourage students to find examples in their research that link geographic location to commercial activity.*

Geography and History Activity 15, pp. 29–30

1. Climate, soil, landforms, and other physical features affect the natural vegetation and animal life of a region as well as which crops can be cultivated.
2. People may irrigate land in order to grow food, they may remove naturally occurring vegetation such as trees or grasses in order to grow crops, and their crops may change the quality of the soil. Removal of forest or grasslands will affect the animals found in a region. People might also build roads or trails to facilitate trade.
3. The cold climate and frozen soil were not suitable for farming.
4. Farming is a stationary practice, so people were able to survive in one place. Bison moved from place to place, so people who lived on bison had to follow them.
5. The types of dwellings people build, the types of clothing they wear, and the kinds of symbols used in their religion are all examples of aspects of culture that could be affected by geography.
6. A people's history, trading partners, personality of leaders, and technology are all examples of other things that can affect culture.
7. *Results will vary but should provide information about Native Americans who lived in the area and how the geography and natural resources affected their diet and dwellings. If the people lived in permanent settlements, they changed the environment by building structures; if farmers, they changed it by removing some vegetation. If they were hunter-gatherer bands, they may not have changed the geography.*

Geography and History Activity 16, pp. 31–32

1. As humans move themselves or goods from one place to another, they create paths or routes between those places. The places where goods are traded become market centers. Specialized commercial support activities also grow up in these market centers.
2. Venice's monopoly on Mediterranean trade made it a center for shipbuilding, banking, and maritime-supply industries that outfitted ships for long voyages.
3. The Grand Canal provided a main thoroughfare for commercial traffic throughout Venice. Wider than any of the other canals in the city, the Grand Canal accommodated a large number of boats.
4. Venice was located midway between Asian markets and western European markets. Located on the Adriatic, Venice was slightly isolated from competitive Mediterranean cities. Thus, Venice could establish its own trading empire without interference from others.
5. The Venetian trafficking of goods across the Mediterranean was similar to the Islamic caravans that brought European goods into sub-Saharan Africa. The Venetians served as intermediaries between the Islamic spice traders and the western European merchants. In a similar way, Islamic merchants served as intermediaries between the western European merchants and the Ghanaian kings who controlled all the gold that flowed in and out of their kingdom.
6. *Possible answers:* war, famine, or other natural disasters; quest for political or religious freedom; desire to live in a different climate; opportunity to initiate trade in an area that had once been closed to trade
7. *Provide several classroom atlases. Encourage students to use current almanacs, nonfiction books, or geographic magazines to do their research on contemporary trade centers.*

Geography and History Activity 17, pp. 33–34

1. Absolute location identifies exact locations using a grid such as latitude and longitude; relative location compares one location to another location without a grid.
2. west of the Canary Islands; one of 723 Bahamian islands farthest to the northeast of Cuba
3. 23°09'00"N latitude and 73°29'13"W longitude
4. land is to the S, SW, and NW of San Salvador; physical features of island
5. descriptions of other islands that can be identified by geographic features

6. Navigators used the compass to determine direction. Knowing the water's depth could help prevent ships from running aground.
7. Knowing the length of the rope, Columbus could calculate the speed his boat was traveling. By multiplying this speed by the number of hours underway, he could calculate the distance.
8. *Answers might include any of the explorers discussed in this chapter. Be sure students discuss the effects of exploration on Europeans and the native peoples contacted.*

Geography and History Activity 18, pp. 35–36

1. Because any feature that is common throughout an area can define a region, regions can take almost any shape or size depending on the common feature that defines them.
2. The power of the regions was determined by the political control of the shogun.
3. The law of the shogun proclaimed that traitors should be expelled from their domains and that no outsider should be allowed to live in any domain.
4. The main part of the shogun's region was located in the center of Japan and divided north from south. Other parts of the shogun's region were located throughout the country and thus served to separate daimyos domains from one another.
5. If the customs of a domain were secret, any outsider or fugitive criminal who came into the domain would quickly give himself away. He would then be caught and expelled, preventing him from establishing a conspiracy.
6. Facilities were required to support this frequent travel. Inns, workers producing means of transport, and the merchants supplying them all benefited from the increased travel.
7. *Examples include:* Romans versus barbarian regions, Muslim versus non-Muslim regions, and Protestant versus Catholic regions. Within American history, the Civil War is an example of a conflict between regions—North against South.

Geography and History Activity 19, pp. 37–38

1. *Answers will vary.* Humans alter their environment not only to accommodate their immediate needs for food, clothing, and shelter but also for a variety of other reasons, such as to protect their land from ocean surges, to improve agricultural land, to modify land for residential or commercial purposes, and to provide open spaces for recreational or environmental uses.
2. The Netherlands has miles of beaches that face the North Sea. Storms ate away at this coastal strip. Fearing the North Sea would break through the beaches and flood their farmland, the Dutch built dikes to hold back the sea.
3. Between 1200 and 1500, Dutch farmers reclaimed only the amount of land they were able to cultivate. The rate of land reclamation was the same for 300 years.
4. The Netherlands controlled Asian spice trade and opened new commercial ports throughout the world. Their maritime superiority brought great wealth to the country. Growing populations required new land for agriculture, which accounts for the increase in land reclamation at that time.
5. *Possible answers:* The Dutch would have more recreational areas available for personal enjoyment; natural environmental areas would be protected from industrial development; a balance could exist between urban and rural environments.
6. *Students may want to work in cooperative-learning groups to brainstorm their ideas about human-environment interaction. Have each group appoint a leader who can oversee group members as they contribute to the research and writing of a group report.*

Geography and History Activity 20, pp. 39–40

1. because they have different viewpoints and perceptions of an area
2. It was the "greatest" planet in the universe.
3. his studies of the movement of planets in the universe
4. He could have been punished for disagreeing with Church teachings.
5. *Answers will vary. Possible answer:* If a person is new to the area, he or she will not know local landmarks.
6. He started people thinking in new ways. Eventually this new thinking led to the breakdown of the "old order" of thinking.
7. *Answers will vary. Possible answer:* Institutions can often shape the way people think about places in the world through the policies, teachings, or statements they present. For example, during war situations, governments often present the opposing government and country as being inherently evil.
8. *Answers will vary. Possible answer:* If the directions given are overly broad or vague, you can assume the direction-givers know little about world geography.

Geography and History Activity 21, pp. 41–42

1. People's perceptions of regions are influenced by their experiences, by the knowledge they have about a land and its people, and by political motivations or restrictions.
2. Spanish: mineral wealth—gold and silver; French: furs; English: rich land for farming
3. England's climate is wet and cool, not the best for growing a wide variety of crops. Discovering the mild climate and rich soil in Virginia, the English were eager to set up agricultural colonies that could supply the homeland with food.
4. Because of the popularity of beaver hats in Europe, beaver furs commanded a high price. French traders made good profits from the fur-trading business in North America.
5. When the pope divided the Atlantic Ocean between the Spanish and the Portuguese in 1493 by setting

the line of demarcation, most of North and South America fell to Spain.
6. The English wanted to capture the large quantities of gold and silver carried on Spanish ships.
7. *Supply students with resources such as almanacs, non-fiction books, and geographic magazines. Encourage them to share their perceptions of the same region with the rest of the class.*

Geography And History Activity 22, pp. 43–44
1. mountains, deserts, climate, laws
2. 800 miles; approximately 3 months
3. more than 400,000 troops
4. Modern barriers are more likely to be repressive governments and immigration laws than geographical features.
5. Russian people were probably severely hurt by the destruction. *Possible answer:* Leaders feel that it is better to destroy their land and goods and suffer the consequences than to be taken over by an enemy country.
6. *Possible answers:* Hinder: prohibits flow of people and ideas that could help to improve the nation. Help: prohibits warfare with other countries that could damage the nation.
7. *Answers should reflect an understanding of the geographic theme of the movement.*

Geography and History Activity 23, pp. 45–46
1. Settlers usually tried to transform the environment to meet their needs.
2. to link the Great Lakes with the Atlantic Ocean
3. New York wilderness, the difference in elevation between Lake Erie and the Hudson River
4. He was convinced that the development and trade the canal would bring to New York would justify the effort and the expense.
5. Industry prospered because goods could be transported faster and more cheaply; the success of the Erie Canal probably convinced other areas to build canals.
6. The British began their canal systems before the Americans did. *Possible questions:* What were some of the biggest geographical problems you encountered? How did you solve them? What types of equipment did you use? How many workers were needed to complete the projects?
7. *Answers will vary. Possible answer:* Cultures have different attitudes toward the land. Some do not feel that they have the right to alter their natural surroundings.
8. *Answers will vary. Possible answers include:* new highways or other major projects such as oil pipelines to Alaska

Geography and History Activity 24, pp. 47–48
1. physical characteristics and human characteristics
2. the size of the population, the population growth rate, the population density, and the distribution of people within the place; *Answers will vary. Possible answers:* town hall, U.S. Census Bureau
3. the developing nations of the world; There will probably be food shortages.
4. Malthus felt that the population was going to outstrip the food supply.
5. Many people in richer countries have more food than they need; in fact, more than half are overweight. In addition, countries like the United States produce more food than they eat. This could be given or sold to poorer countries, not destroyed.
6. *Answers will vary. Possible answer:* Education can help people to learn how to limit the size of their families; education produces technological advances that help to increase food supplies.
7. *Answers will vary.* Reports may look at the use of technology, new crop strains, financing, and storage.

Geography and History Activity 25, pp. 49–50
1. physical factors and human factors
2. Australia began as a convict colony to relieve overcrowding in British prisons.
3. People discovered Australia's rich natural resources—pastureland and gold.
4. *Answers will vary, but students should explain that it was the pioneering work of the first convicts who drilled for water, built the railroads, and cleared the land for settlement. Students should understand that native inhabitants are ignored in this poem.*
5. It suggests that the British people thought the lives of prisoners were expendable. *Most students will probably disagree with this attitude. They should give reasons for why they disagree with the British policy.*
6. The Australians probably look on their past with a sense of good humor and acceptance. Australians have developed an independent spirit sometimes compared to the pioneers of the American West. Some Australians may still hold grudges against Great Britain for its past colonialist attitudes.
7. *Encourage students to include examples in their answers.*

Geography and History Activity 26, pp. 51–52
1. the background of the person giving the description, including the values, attitudes, and perceptions that affected his or her estimate of the place
2. Catherine Wilmot considered only the material happiness of the Russian serfs. Unlike Herzen, she did not consider matters of higher value such as freedom of the individual, both because such things may not have been as important to her and because it may not have occurred to her that serfs deserved them.
3. Wilmot chose for her comparison a country where the peasants were worse off than the Russian serfs. This supported her claim that the serfs lived well. Herzen chose Europe, where the value placed on

individual freedom was high, which supported his claim that in Russia it was difficult to live with dignity.
4. *One might have expected both observers to view the peasants as better off than they really were, due to lack of familiarity with their conditions.*
5. *Answers may include a feeling that such hard labor should be performed by machines.*
6. *Answers may point to Herzen's analysis: The Russian peasant was completely swallowed up by the state and never even tried to escape it. Without any understanding of the concept of individual freedom, peasants may have felt threatened by any proposed change of their status as property of the landowners.*
7. *Essays should reflect the current status of individual freedom in Russia, as documented by newspaper items.*

Geography and History Activity 27, pp. 53–54
1. They wanted to transport goods across India.
2. They brought the Indian people closer together.
3. English made it easier for Indians who spoke different languages to communicate with each other.
4. Pramathanath initially admired British culture. He wore European clothes and was proud that the British invited him to take the train ride.
5. He realized that the British were bigoted against his fellow Indians; he realized that the British judged him favorably only because he was dressed like them, in European clothes.
6. *Answers will vary. Some students might say that, in retrospect, it was unwise of Britain to improve India's transportation and communication because those improvements ultimately led to India's independence. Other students may say that improving transportation and communication were essential for the British to manage India, so it was a wise decision regardless of the outcome.*
7. *Answers will vary. Students might note more ecologically responsible forms of transportation, such as increased use of bicycles and mass transit, and research into fuels made of corn or other less toxic substances. The Internet and the World Wide Web make global communication more accessible. Improvements in transportation help conserve the earth's natural resources. Improvements in communication bring people from all over the world closer together.*
8. *Answers will vary. Students who agree with the statement might mention that television enables a vast number of people to see films, theatrical performances, operas, concerts, and sporting events that they cannot attend in person. Students disagreeing might cite television's violence, its many commercials, and the low intellectual level of much of the programming.*

Geography and History Activity 28, pp. 55–56
1. Each group interacted with the environment in different ways and so perceived it differently.
2. The fertile plains were important to the farmers because they were good for crops.
3. The hills were important to soldiers because they gave commanding views.
4. Farming preserved the environment and encouraged its life-giving properties; warfare destroyed the environment.
5. *Answers will vary. Students might say that modern warfare would cause even greater damage to the environment because of the use of nuclear, chemical, or biological weapons.*
6. *Answers will vary. Students might say that factory owners would be interested in harnessing the power of the river and building factories on the plains.*
7. *Answers will vary. Students might say that the armies were transforming a wooded, fertile valley into a desolate and barren wasteland.*
8. *Encourage students to answer the questions by using appropriate reference materials.*

Geography and History Activity 29, pp. 57–58
1. Tailors can find many customers in urban areas.
2. In the open areas of eastern Europe, the Jews were primarily agricultural.
3. Both the street musicians and the tailor walked around the streets and sold their wares. The musicians sold music and the tailor sold clothes.
4. *Answers will vary. Students might say that the Germans were jealous of the Jews' material success and hated their unfamiliar culture.*
5. *Answers will vary. Students might say that community members work in local farms or mines and hike on local hills.*
6. *Answers will vary. Students might say that as people exert more control over their environment and as transportation improves, location's role diminishes.*
7. *Answers will vary. Possible answers: The city should be built in a central location that could serve as a transportation hub and encourage industry.*
8. *Answers will vary. Students living near rivers might suggest bottling the water and selling it to water-deprived areas; those living near plains might suggest growing plants that could be distilled into alternative fuels.*

Geography and History Activity 30, pp. 59–60
1. Each community contains several elements, and each of those elements falls into its own region.
2. tribal regions (Masai, Kikuyu, Somali) and the Kenyan political region, among others
3. The European colonists split up Africa without any regard for tribal regions.
4. conflicts among tribes; between tribes and national governments; among national governments
5. He wanted to form a united continent.
6. *Answers will vary. Possible answers: A new map might resolve tribal conflict but encourage international conflict. Instead of forcing people to resolve their conflicts, the new borders might only encourage more conflict.*

7. *Answers will vary. Possible answers:* The community belongs to municipal, county, state, and federal regions. The resulting bureaucracy can be either helpful or harmful.
8. *Answers will vary. Possible maps might show how forming Palestinian and Kurdish states could resolve conflicts in the Middle East.*

Geography and History Activity 31, pp. 61–62

1. Evaluating barriers to movement can disclose an enemy's weakness during war or reveal causes and effects to historians.
2. The barrier of sea distances prevented the Japanese from readily supplying their industry with materials, their war machine with fuels, and their population with food. The Allies' exploitation of this difficulty with a blockade was one of the major factors which led to the Japanese surrender.
3. *Answers may suggest that imports from Korea would be the last to be interrupted, because the distance between Japan and Korea is less than the distance between Japan and its other sources of key materials.*
4. The chief cause for the failure of Japanese shipping was destruction by submarines.
5. *Answers should focus on the question of whether Japan was truly "forced" to invade either mainland Asia or the Dutch East Indies; that is, whether other courses of action were available to it.*
6. *Answers should mention that Europe, being a continuous landmass, had no internal sea barriers to invasion after armies had landed on its shores in France and Italy. Allied armies could sweep into the heart of Germany in a relatively short time, especially since the distances involved were much smaller than the distances between Japan and nearby Allied bases. It is clear that the reason Japan was not subject to a destructive land invasion was that it was surrounded by ocean barriers. Thus barriers to movement both helped and hurt Japan's war effort.*
7. *Students may mention that nations that protect their economies with artificial tariffs and quotas inevitably incur retaliation from other nations. The result is that countries waste their own resources because of the artificial prices that result. Japan has a history of protecting steel, automobile, and construction industries, as well as its agriculture.*

Geography and History Activity 32, pp. 63–64

1. geographic regions distinguished by political ideology
2. They saw world politics as a choice between two ideologies, communism and democracy.
3. Some nations disagreed with the bipolar view of the world; they noted the significance of a third group of developing nations not necessarily aligned with either superpower.
4. The Communist bloc had become large and powerful by 1963.
5. *Possible choices include:* South Africa, China, Israel, Great Britain, Mexico, and the former Soviet Union. *Encourage students to consider countries they view favorably as well as those they view negatively.*
6. It was quite successful in halting the flow of people. However, Western fashions, music, and political ideals slowly made their way into the East bloc.
7. *The map might include the member nations of the European Union, as well as some newly democratized East European countries. The capital might be the current EU capital, Brussels, or students might want to relocate it to another major city. Arguments in favor of such an alliance include the easing of trade restrictions, the creation of a common currency, and the increased global power such a country would wield. Note that the plans for European unity are discussed in detail in Chapter 35.*

Geography and History Activity 33, pp. 65–66

1. It has a large population, a capitalist economy, and is an important seaport.
2. Its location and excellent harbor encouraged people to become engaged in trading and finance.
3. They have built crowded cities near the water.
4. The history and economic systems of Hong Kong and China are different. Years of British rule in Hong Kong created a society that is based on Western-style, capitalist values. China, on the other hand, has a Communist system.
5. They fear the imposition of a Communist economy and lifestyle and the possible loss of their jobs, freedoms, and wealth.
6. Its physical proximity to Vietnam; Hong Kong's thriving industries offered job opportunities; people also sought the political freedom and stability found there. The refugees eventually strained Hong Kong's resources and increased the level of poverty.
7. *Before students begin, have them make a list, orally or on paper, of the qualities of place that Hong Kong possesses. Then ask students to consider whether a new location would affect each quality.*

Geography and History Activity 34, pp. 67–68

Answers may vary but should be similar to the following:
1. Apartheid means "apartness," and restricting people's movement ensured that the races stayed apart.
2. Restricting the movement of the Bantu ensured that the majority of the population was always under control. As people were not able to move freely, it may have been more difficult for the Bantu population to mobilize against apartheid on a large scale.
3. *Some students may feel that it would have been difficult for the South African government to control the Bantu indefinitely because the majority of the population are Bantu. Others might feel that, in the absence of global pressure, the white minority could have controlled the Bantu majority indefinitely because the whites had access to the country's weapons and economic resources.*
4. Throughout history, such restrictions have been used by one group of people to oppress another. Two examples of peoples oppressed in this way are the slaves in the Middle Passage and the Jewish prison-

ers of the Holocaust. The less free people are to move, the less social freedom they have.
5. *Reports should indicate an understanding that, although economic pressures and the threat of physical violence throughout this period made life difficult everywhere in the country, life in the homelands was much poorer and had fewer opportunities than life in white South Africa.*

Geography and History Activity 35, pp. 69–70
1. increased air pollution (including smog, carbon dioxide, poisonous gases), soot and ash deposits
2. The long-term effects are often unknown or immeasurable, as is the length of time needed for recovery.
3. *Answers include:* damage to beaches, wetlands, desalinization plants, sea life, and the floor of the gulf.
4. Much more attention is usually paid to the human, political, and economic outcomes of war, and the environmental effects are often not immediately known.
5. *Answers will vary. Negative effects might include:* the devastation of French land between the trenches (No Man's Land) during World War I, the atomic bombings of Hiroshima and Nagasaki, deforestation of Vietnam during the Vietnam War, nuclear testing at Bikini Atoll, the Chernobyl nuclear disaster, or the Exxon *Valdez* oil spill. *Positive effects might include:* restoration work after natural disasters such as earthquakes and floods, legislation to set aside land for national parks, efforts to save the Brazilian rain forest, and antipollution legislation.
6. *Provide students with a simple world map on which the Himalayas are marked. If further information is available about specific areas affected by the disaster, have students find and mark the locations on the map.*

Geography and History Activity 36, pp. 71–72
1. It is the result of factors that push people out of one area and pull them toward another.
2. The move to the cities, shown on the left, boosts Mexico City's population, shown on the right.
3. the excitement of the city and the presence of friends and relatives there
4. Many of the new arrivals live in camps without water and sewer services, which are strained to the limits. They also contribute to the increase in cars and therefore smog. The overcrowding has added to crime problems, the buildup of garbage, and the spread of disease.
5. *Answers will vary. Students might suggest creating more employment opportunities in rural areas and other, less-crowded cities.*
6. Similar migration would be expected in countries with severe poverty and unemployment among farmers.
7. *Prompt students to explore the city's architecture, arts, foods, and religious and historical sites.*

Geography and History Activity 37, pp. 73–74
1. They include weather patterns, the composition of the oceans, and the food chain. Systems such as these can be greatly affected by human alteration of the environment.
2. Asia and Africa
3. Groeneveld attempts to meet the human problems that are the cause of the environmental damage.
4. Rain forests provide much of the oxygen we breathe.
5. The earth's ecosystem is far larger and more complex than people had imagined; the rain forests are a crucial part of that ecosystem.
6. It could adopt harsher measures against them or find alternative farming methods and other types of jobs for the campesinos.
7. *The reports should pursue the following reasoning:* Despite the immense variety of species in the forests, none is superfluous—each occupies a niche in the food chain. In addition, the plant and insect life protect and support each other. So disruption of the rain forest could upset the ecological balance, thereby threatening insects, animals, and trees. This could affect not only specific areas but also the balance of the world's ecosystems.

ACKNOWLEDGMENTS

Text

57 From "American Food Crops in the Old World" by William H. McNeill from *Seeds of Change: A Quincentennial Commemoration* edited by Herman J. Viola and Carolyn Margolis, copyright © 1991 by the Smithsonian Institution.

65 From "Waiting for China" by Andrew Cockburn. *Condé Nast Traveler*, (August 1993).

67 Mosima Gabriel Sexwale and Van Zyl Slabbert, as quoted in, *Illustrated History of South Africa: The Real Story*, copyright © 1988, 1989 by The Reader's Digest Association, Inc.

Photographs

5 Scala/Art Resource, NY
19 Vann/Art Resource, NY
21 Robert Azzi/Woodfin Camp
29 Barry L. Runk/Grant Heilman Photography, Inc.
31 Scala/Art Resource, NY
39 The Bettmann Archive
45 The Bettmann Archive
51 Scala/Art Resource, NY
53 Bettmann/Hulton
55 The Bettmann Archive
57 Alter Kaazyne Yivo Institute for Jewish Research
65 R. Chen/SuperStock

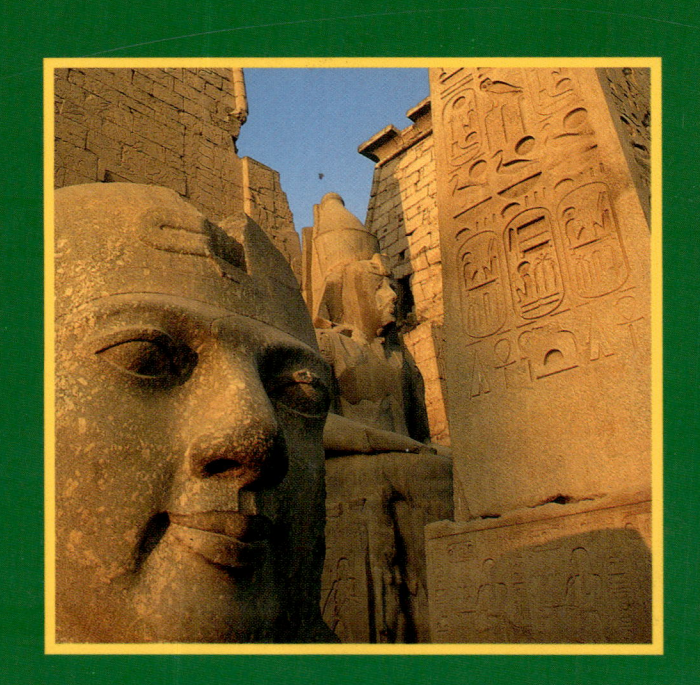

ISBN 0-02-823225-9

GLENCOE
McGraw-Hill